BEYOND REASON:

SONGWRITING ON PURPOSE

BEYOND REASON: SONGWRITING ON PURPOSE

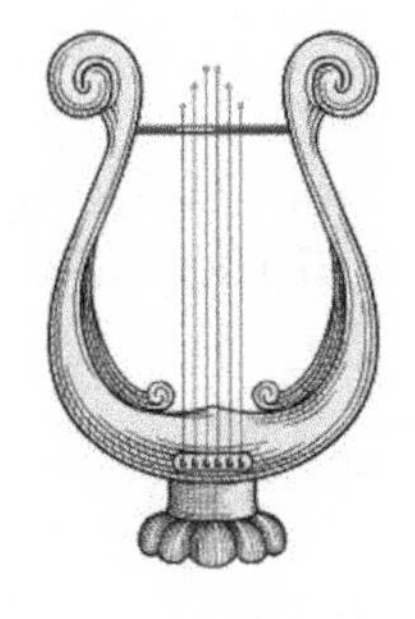

BY
JANE ROSS FALLON

BEYOND REASON: SONGWRITING ON PURPOSE

A Guide To Using Classical Rhetoric To Write Songs That Say What You Want Them To Say

Published by Town Forest Books and Music
82 Pepperell Road, Brookline, NH 03033

Library of Congress Control Number:
2016917836

Cover Design by Jane Fallon
Aristotle image courtesy of Wikimedia Commons

Fallon, Jane, 1953 –
Beyond Reason: Songwriting On Purpose/Jane Fallon
Includes bibliographical references
ISBN: 978-0-692-79692-4
1. Book 2. Poetry 3.Written Work

Table of Contents

PREFACE

What is Writing Beyond Reason?

"You don't write because you want to say something, you write because you have something to say."

F. Scott Fitzgerald

Most people begin with a "reason" for writing and feel that much songwriting comes from the personal; we think of song-writing as something sacred, stemming from deep revelations and providing personal or communal healing.

This is often the case. But there are times when the message of the song, the purpose, is the true goal. To write purposefully requires going beyond the reason and utilizing specific skills that make sure that purpose is accomplished..

It is in this type of songwriting that we truly learn to understand the well-known quote (attributed to several people) that says approximately this: "Creativity is 1% inspiration and 99% perspiration." Writing purposefully is a craft. How can song-writing be a "craft"? We usually associate that term with the making of a tangible product, however the definition of the verb is simply to "exercise skill in making something." Writing songs for a purpose requires a special set of skills, and there are classic tools we can use to 'craft' songs that go "beyond reason". The song that makes a point to go beyond personal revelation is the hardest to write. But the tools are there to help us, and they have been there for over 2,000 years. You know most of this already, but perhaps you just haven't put names to all of it.

There are 2,714 books about songwriting listed on Amazon.com at this particular moment. By the time anyone reads this, there will most likely be many more. Brian Austin Whitney of the organization "Just Plain Folks" has said, "There are more songwriters than there are people." What is this attraction to songwriting? I could attempt an answer, but it would take another book.

Songwriting is obviously a popular topic, and different ways of approaching it abound. A great many of these books probe aspects of the technical craft, such as how to write good lyrics, and melodies. In addition, they might examine the technical toolkit of song forms and organizational structures. Some of these books are about how to write that "hit" song or how to "make it" in the music business. Many writers seem to struggle with "writer's block"; they don't know what to write or how to proceed, and teachers offer ways to find inspiration and direction. Other books help "hone" the product and offer suggestions for getting out of the rut. There is an approach for everyone.

There are those who question if songwriting can be taught. A quick "Google" search of the phrase "can songwriting be taught" produced 6,400,000 results. I did not examine all of them, (lazy, I know) but it is easy to understand that the question of "talent" vs. "skills" frequently emerges. Some see the process as organic, depending on inspiration and innate creativity, and something given to some and not others. Others advocate for the "everyone can do it" approach.

What kinds of individuals "teach" songwriting? Songwriting is usually "taught" by those who have credentials of some kind. These credentials might be the number of hit songs they have written or contests they have won. Or, they may have written several articles on the subjects that have been published in respected magazines. Unlike traditional academic subjects, songwriting does not usually offer a typical academic approach. One can acquire a PhD in music composition, which might include lyricism and popular song craft, and many academic treatises on the folk ballad or cultural genre have been written.

Bath Spa University in England claims to offer the world's first and only Master's degree in songwriting, although I also found a degree for Songwriting and Performance at the University of the West of Scotland. There may be more springing up as I write this.

I find this dichotomy highly provocative. There are two Master's degrees on Songwriting in the world at this moment, and approximately 3,000 books on the subject. What that tells me is that songwriting, removed from the established studies of Composition, is something that one does not need a degree to do. All it seems to require is passion.

What other kinds of individuals teach songwriting? Perhaps the best teachers are those whose songwriting you like and whose songwriting inspires you. Songwriting has some established parameters that have been used successfully throughout the history of music that can indeed be taught, however, the larger history of popular songwriting has been one of the street, the back porch, the farm, the road, etc.

What all of these grassroots songs have in common is that they arose from a human desire to communicate for a reason through the powerful medium of music. For some, that reason became something even larger. It sprang from a purpose. For those who already write songs, this book is not meant to change the way you approach songwriting. Some of you prefer to build from the ground up, establishing chord progressions, fiddling with melody riffs and tempos. Others start with a lyric or an idea.

Writer David McCullough noted, "Writing is thinking. To write well is to think clearly. That's why it is so hard." As an instructor of English Composition, I have often faced the overwhelming task of teaching a class of freshman students to write on a college level. They have come from a variety of school settings and have varying degrees of writing ability. They often say things like "I am bad at grammar," "I never could spell," or "I tend to write fragments." I tell them that these are issues that need to be worked on, but they are not what writing is about.

Those are editing issues. I usually tell them that writing is a life-long skill and that while I might not be able to make them into great writers in one semester, by golly, maybe I can teach them to think.

What are some "purposes" for writing"? Except for special occasions or entertainment, there are only two reasons for communicating: to inform and to persuade. This book is not intended to teach you "how to write a hit song", or craft a better lyric, or break writer's block. These subjects are covered well by many skilled songwriting teachers. Rather, I hope that it will serve as a tool to "think better." If we understand the "how" and the "why", we can better shape our songs to suit the purpose that we intend for them, whether that is to inform, persuade, or entertain. It is through understanding the classic modes of development and their relationship to your audience that you can best develop the content that achieves your purpose.

Songwriting has special issues that include musicality and performance. However, the writing process is all the same no matter what the medium; it is about making a conscious effort to understand your purpose and audience. It is emotion, it is inspiration and it is a craft. In this book, we will examine that craft to see what tools are needed in order to write songs that go "beyond reason" to achieve your special purpose.

After all, what is a great song? For most of us, it is one that achieves what it is we want it to achieve.

.

PART I: STANDING ON THE SHOULDERS OF GIANTS

"Excellence is never an accident. It is always the result of high intention, sincere effort, and intelligent execution; it represents the wise choice of many alternatives – choice, not chance, determines your destiny."

~ Aristotle

THE RHETORICAL RHOMBUS AND THE MODES OF DEVELOPMENT

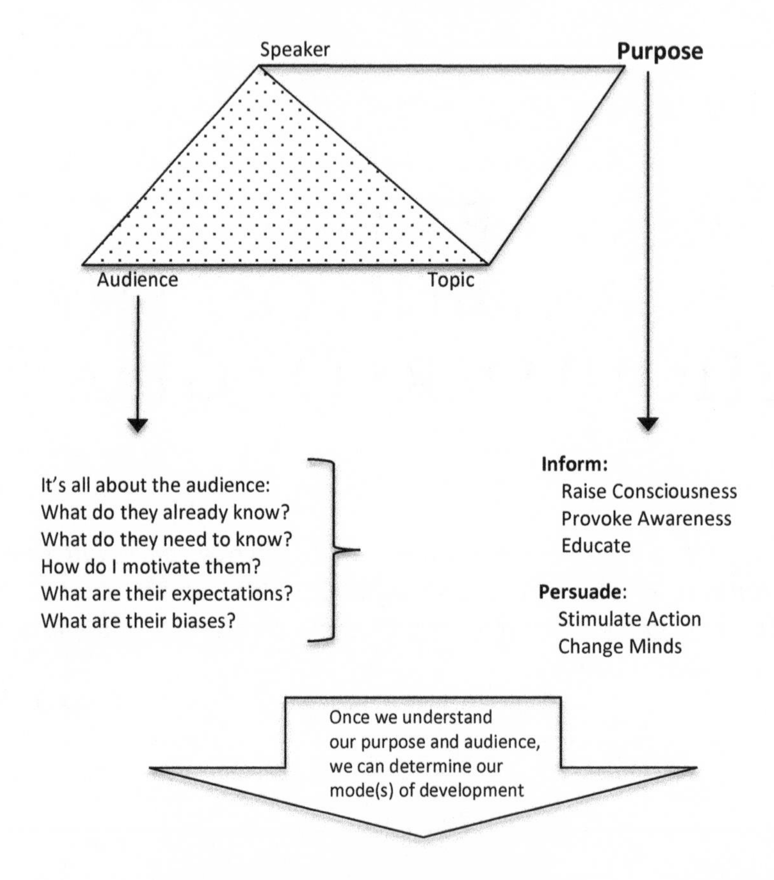

Narration: describes who, what, when, where
Description: appeals to the five senses
Illustration: provides examples
Cause and Effect: explains the causes and results
Classification and Division: divides situations into smaller parts
Comparison and Contrast: explains how things are the same or different
Definition: makes terms and ideas understandable
Process Analysis: explains how something happened.

REINVENTING THE WHEEL

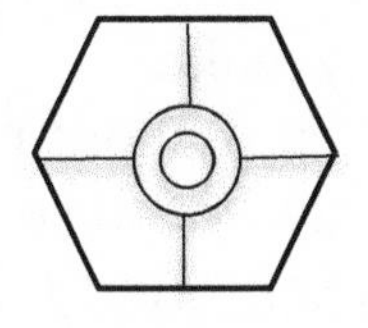 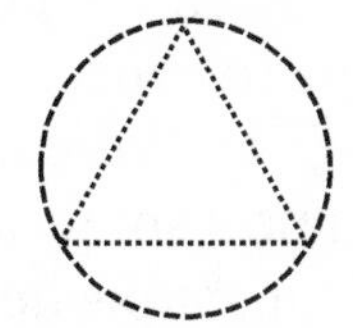 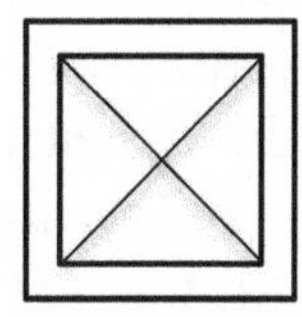

I think in I shall "reinvent the wheel". Let's see, I will make it square. Then I will take out all but 2 spokes. And I shall use glass instead of wood or steel. Voila! I have reinvented the wheel. But is it still a wheel? Does it work like it should?

Don't you love clichés? They usually come from somewhere important and say something with universal application or they would not become clichés. The wheel has been used as an example of the perfect invention, however, that doesn't mean it hasn't been added to and adapted. People are manipulating the wheel all of the time.

While the very first form can't be re-invented, we can build on the example set by that very first wheel. Perfect in shape, the wheel revolutionized transport, irrigation, milling and pottery making. But even the wheel wasn't perfect for all occasions. Sometimes mountain goats are more effective than wheels. Sometimes wheels aren't necessary at all because a specific endeavor does not require a wheel.

For some uses, it can be improved upon. Currently, someone has invented a double-helix-shaped skateboard wheel that seems to take on those rough cracks and bumps of today's riders better than round heels. (www.sharkwheel.com) However, it is still a wheel, and its origin stems from those basic premises that caused the wheel to be designed in the first place.

What does this have to do with songwriting? Well, we can adapt the tools of the past deliberately, or we can create with abandon, giving little heed to those who have gone before – if that is even possible. We are all pretty much shaped by ages of traditions; they permeate our everyday existence, whether we know it or not, and thank goodness for that. With those tools available to us, we can concentrate on the job of communicating much more readily. These tools help songwriters especially when they are writing "on purpose" – when they have a specific point that they hope to consciously make.

One of the nicest things I have overheard about my songwriting is the following: "Jane's songs always mean so much." I have written my share of fun, superficial songs but I do admit to being drawn to making a point and shaping my songs around meaningful content. The song that makes a point to go beyond personal revelation is the hardest to write. But the tools are there to help us, and they have been there for over 2,000 years.

These tools will be recognizable to you. You encounter them everyday, but you just haven't put a name to them yet. Each of these tools, alone and in combination, help us communicate. Most likely, we have a point to make when we communicate – we have a purpose.

That takes us to a guy named Aristotle. He was a famous Greek philosopher born in 384 BC. You know that song *It's All Been Done* by Steven Page and recorded by Barenaked Ladies? Well, you would not have found Aristotle humming anything of the sort because he was too busy doing it. Aristotle transformed everything he touched and very often he was first. He was first to classify disciplines like Mathematics and Biology, and he was first to develop a formalized structure for reasoning. In his time he was known as "the man who knew everything". (Ah, to have tons of free time and loads of slaves. Just kidding. We'd like to think it was that easy.) It takes a special mind to reflect on things that shape the future in the way that Aristotle, Plato, and Socrates did.

The great Greek philosopher laid the foundation for everything any writer needs to know about discourse, especially persuasive discourse. He called it "rhetoric" and it set a standard for all subsequent communication. His book, *Rhetoric,* is very complicated and requires hours of study, but for our purpose we can distill it to what is known as the rhetorical triangle and to the persuasive appeals.

The following triangle was first developed by a literary scholar named Robert Scholes[1] as an adaptation of Aristotle's rhetorical triangle, which will be addressed fully later in this work. The rhetorical triangle sets out the main aspects of all communication:

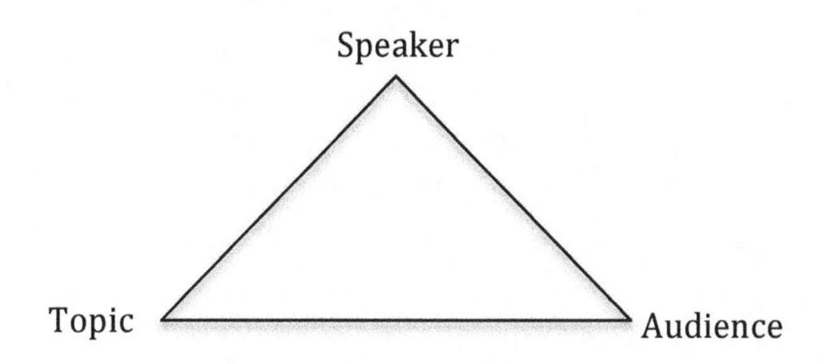

In Aristotle's world, where most discourse was spoken, and where most spoken word had the purpose of creating change in society, Aristotle automatically considered rhetoric to be persuasive. Therefore, his triangle omits a fourth concern that has been added to the contemporary approach to communication which makes it a "rhetorical rhombus".[2] The rhombus includes the "aim" or "purpose" for the discourse. This purpose does not have to be persuasive or argumentative in nature, but rather it simply constitutes a specific goal that the songwriter has for his/her topic.

The phrase, "we stand on the shoulders of giants" is a modern version of one made most famous by Sir Isaac Newton (1676) who said, "If I have seen further, it is by standing on the shoulders of giants."

However, the image of dwarfs perched on the shoulders of giants goes back to Greek mythology (those Greeks again!). We are the dwarfs my friend, and that gives us a great viewpoint.

Why reinvent the wheel? Why not perch on the shoulders of giants and use those tools that they came up with? Do what you want with them to give yourself voice.

It has all been done – just not by you.

PART II: DUSTING OFF YOUR SOUL

The purpose of art is washing the dust of daily life off our souls.

~Pablo Picasso

Efforts and courage are not enough without purpose and direction.

~John F. Kennedy

It is important as a songwriter to realize that your topic is not your purpose. Your reason can be a purpose, or it can just simply be an impetus. Real purpose is an objective or intention. To achieve this we must fully examine what it is we want to achieve and make choices that enable us to craft that purpose.

We often think of reason and purpose as being the same thing, however, there are differences between them. Except for special-occasion speeches or for simple entertainment, people communicate to either inform or persuade. The "reason" we write can be as simple as to explain an idea, convey an emotion, or analyze a situation. Within the rhetorical triangle, reason explains the speaker's connection to his/her topic. Sometimes a reason is really impetus – a force that begins the writing process, such an emotional upheaval, or the desire to write for a song prompt, a contest, or a special occasion. For some it is a job. Cole Porter said, "My sole inspiration is a telephone call from a producer."[3] Inspiration of any kind might be what sparks the fire, but it is not the purpose of the production.

When one writes with a purpose, one goes beyond reason. Purpose indicates the aim or intention of the speakers. Purposeful writing sets a specific goal for the topic. The purpose of a song indicates the connection between the speaker and his/her audience, that fourth aspect of rhetoric that completes the rhombus.

Most songwriters will have a general idea of the purpose of their writing, even if it isn't something that they have delved deeply into. Sometimes that purpose wants simply to inform. Often the songwriter wants to just relate a story, set a scene, or create a feeling that the audience might understand. That sort of purpose might be secondary to the impetus for writing the song and includes such stimulus as a broken relationship, a death of a friend, or the birth of a new love.

The difference between reason and purpose:

Reason (Impetus): I am sad.
Purpose: Writing a song will make me feel better.

Larger Purpose: This song will make everyone feel better.

Reason (Impetus): My father died.
Purpose: I want to record my father's interesting life.
Larger Purpose: There are things everyone can learn from my father.

Reason (impetus): We have an Earth Day in my community.
Purpose: There is potential damage to our town if the pipeline is completed.
Larger Purpose: I want to make everyone understand that the pipeline is dangerous to the environment at large.

What is it that we are actually trying to achieve with our purpose? Well, persuasion could include any number of words: persuade, convince, influence, argue, recommend, change, advocate, urge, defend, justify, or support.

We can inform, describe, define, review, notify, instruct, advise, announce, explain, demonstrate or illustrate.[4] These words may seem like synonyms, but they often require different processes and different techniques.

And so it seems, that along with the dust that comes off our souls, we need a little effort and courage in order to find purpose and direction. Mostly, we need a real understanding of our audience. For what is communication without audience? Without an audience, Aristotle's triangle would just be a line.

PART III: THE ADMIRERS AND THE WATCHERS

You've got a song you're singing from your gut; you want that audience to feel it in their gut. And you've got to make them think that you're one of them sitting out there with them too. They've got to be able to relate to what you're doing.
~Johnny Cash

It requires wisdom to understand wisdom: the music is nothing if the audience is deaf.
~Walter Lippmann

It's the admirer and the watcher who provoke us to all the inanities we commit.
~Seneca

I watched the singer as he sang passionately about his lost love with eyes closed. This, I think, is the "all about me" moment. Now, there is nothing wrong with going into yourself on stage to convey your pain or passion. Certainly you want an audience that will listen and sympathize and it will appreciate your passion. It is much better than singing to the wall in your bedroom.

However, in this instance, the audience is a vague presence. You leave it up to those listening to find that personal connection to them, and when a song is performed with passion that often happens.

However, when one writes with a purpose, the audience becomes even more important than it might in a song that does not have a definite purpose. When you sing a song with a definite goal in mind, you are always "all about the audience." You think about its reaction and hope that your point is getting across. If we don't reach the audience, we have failed to convey our purpose.

And so, we get back to that triangle we discussed earlier. Aristotle lays out an approach to the issue of audience in his *Rhetoric* as well. He stipulates that there are three "appeals" through which we engage our audience. At this point we expand our triangle and include the appeals:

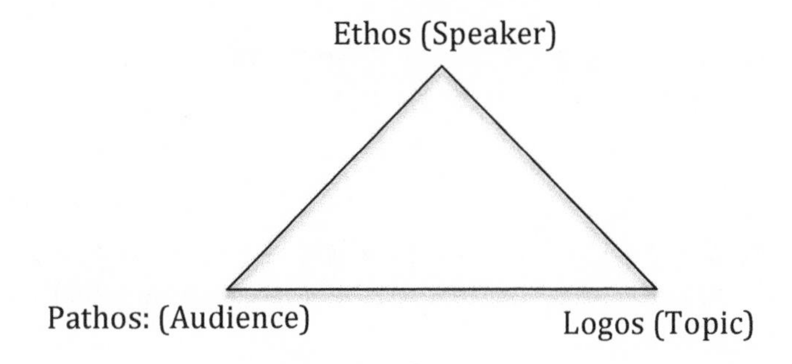

These three appeals can be used together or separately to convey our purpose. Aristotle calls these the "intrinsic" (coming from within) proofs, in contrast to the "extrinsic" (motivated from the outside) proofs.

He felt that both types of proof are needed in persuasion. While the extrinsic proof relies on the concrete, such as statistics, laws, testimony, the intrinsic proofs rely on the art of the speaker.

These proofs are summed up in his three appeals:

Put simply, **Logos** is the appeal to the audience's reason, **Ethos**, the appeal of one's character and **Pathos**, the appeal to the audience's emotion.

Logos: Logic appeals to our audience's reasoning powers. Logic is not statistics or quotes from authorities. Logic stresses our ability to draw conclusions based on assumptions. Most arguments are based on probability and not truth. I don't have to appeal to logic to convince my audience that the world is round and revolves around the sun because they would accept that as truth. However, I will have to outline logical assumptions and convince my audience that these are likely to be true.

There are two types of reasoning:

Deductive (specific to general) states what would be considered generally approved premises in order to draw a conclusion.

Example:

Premise: The earth's average temperature has risen by 1.5 degrees for the past century. Because of this, the polar ice caps are melting and climate is changing.

Premise: Burning fossil fuels releases greenhouse gases, which warm the atmosphere.

Conclusion: Human behavior affects climate.
Inductive (general to specific) begins with general observations to arrive at a specific conclusion.

Observation 1: In Argentinian farming communities where the product Roundup is used, cancer rates are two to four times the national average.

Observation 2: Comparing two villages, thirty-one percent of residents had a family member with cancer, while only 3 percent of residents in a ranching village without spraying had one.

Observation 3: If parents of children were exposed to Roundup within two years of the child's birth, the chances of having a child with brain cancer doubled.

Conclusion: Roundup causes cancer.

You appeal to logic when you rely on your audience's intelligence and when you offer credible evidence to support your argument. That evidence includes:

FACTS –These are valuable because they are not debatable; they represent established truth.

EXAMPLES –These include events or circumstances that your audience can relate to their lives.

PRECEDENTS –These are specific examples (historical and personal) from the past.

AUTHORITY –The authority must be timely (not outdated), and it must be qualified to judge the topic.

Very often songs use the rhetorical device known as the "enthymeme". In this case, one of the premises needed in order to draw the conclusion is unstated. For instance, in the song

Eve of Destruction we are presented a list of current events. We are asked why, when faced with all of this evidence, we don't believe we are on the eve of destruction. The premise that is unstated, the one we must agree with in order to complete the syllogism, is that these events are destructive elements.

In his song, *Short People*, Randy Newman makes his point by turning this enthymeme back on his audience:

Major Premise: Short people are defective in many ways.
Conclusion: They don't deserve to live.

To believe this one, the audience would have to accept the unstated minor premise that these defects are executable offenses. The use of the enthymeme in this case results in very effective satire.

Inductive reasoning is also more likely to be found than deductive reasoning in song. In his song, *We Didn't Light the Fire*, Billy Joel lists examples from over 100 headlines since 1949 to the time he wrote the song and concludes with "it isn't our fault."

Ethos:

At first glance, it would seem that "ethos", or the singer's ability to convince the audience that he/she is to be listened to, would be a performance issue and not a lyrical one. Certainly, there is an art to presentation and, in Public Speaking, we teach students the art of monitoring their body language, eye contact, and gestures to appear to be trustworthy. An added bonus for those who want to be heard is to have built a reputation of knowledge in the area they are singing about.

However, ethos is also conveyed through the words and details we choose. The audience needs to feel that we are credible. Using correct terminology to show a genuine understanding of our topic is helpful, as is being accurate about people, places, and things that may show up in our songs.

This appeal involves convincing our audience that we are intelligent and can be trusted. Writers cannot simply say to their audience "I can be trusted because I'm smart and a good person." Ethos is perhaps the most difficult criteria to establish; we have to prove ourselves by demonstrating that we understand what we are arguing because we are providing:

our personal experience, or
someone else's personal experience, and
expert support through extensive research, and/or
testimony from recognized authorities in the field

Bruce Springsteen, for instance, became known for his "blue-collar ethos". Audiences believe him because he came from a working class background and his songs ring with truth. For similar reasons, Johnny Cash seems the epitome of first-hand experience when he growls out *Folsom Prison Blues.*

One way to show this authority for a subject you might not have lived is through point of view. The voice can be someone's other than yours, such as occurs in *Angel From Montgomery,* or can be related from a point of omniscience like Mac Davis' *In The Ghetto.* Anyone can sing these songs, and the **ethos** is developed through the lyrical power and not from the artist singing. These examples, of course, are also story songs meant to convey pathos, which brings us to the next topic.

Pathos:

Singer/songwriters love pathos. Because there is only so much time to get one's point across in a song, going for the gut is the quickest way to get to the audience. Most people think with their hearts – at least a first.

We humans are emotional beings. When we introduce pathos in our songs we touch upon our delicate sensations such as pity, sympathy, sorrow and, consequently, try to develop an emotional connection with our audience.

Emotions are part of real life. By using pathos, songwriters bring their narratives, characters and themes closer to that reality. Furthermore, the use of pathos by a debater in an argument appeals to people emotionally making it a powerful tool to convince people and change or reinforce their opinions.

Pathos is usually easy to identify, and the songs mentioned in this book in other contexts use it to create empathy for their cause. *Something in the Rain* speaks of the death and pain caused by pesticides and *In the Ghetto* uses a Mama's tears to create a case against poverty in the inner city.

However, many don't recognize that humor is also pathos and can be used very effectively to convince your audience.

Parody and Satire:

Humor is certainly a way to elicit an emotional response. But using humor for a purpose other than laughter is known as satire. Through such techniques as irony or exaggeration, writers can criticize people or cultures. It is especially effective in the context of contemporary politics and other topical issues.

A very famous example of satire in literature is Jonathan Swift's *A Modest Proposal.* Through extreme exaggeration, likening the British attitude toward, and treatment of, the Irish to the treatment of animals, Swift makes a statement as to the their heartlessness. Songwriters make extensive use of satire.

An example of a song that seems humorous on the surface, but also uses logic, is Tom Lehrer's *Who's Next* about the proliferation of nuclear weapons. Using sly, political references and allusions, Lehrer is making a statement about nuclear proliferation. He mentions the justifications that the U.S. makes for having the bomb, probes the irony in China having the bomb – "They can't wipe us out for at least five years" – and pokes fun at Israel by using the 23rd Psalm. Finally, he is aghast that Alabama might get the bomb. By using exaggeration that is veiled reality, his examples make us smile a little while he makes a political point.

A local favorite and friend, Jon Swenson, is known for his humorous songs. Very often they manage to create very succinct social commentary while tickling the funny bone. For instance, he sends up today's airline passenger regulations in his song, *Airline of our Times*:

I was never one for flying in a great big "air-o-plane"
And now I like it even less since the world has gone insane

Arrive three hours early for a flight that just takes two
'Cause a guy set fire to his underwear and another to his shoe
It's a sign, it's a sign, for an airline of our times
It a sign for an airline of our times
The body scans and pat downs to keep you from killing me
We cannot carry liquids "'cept" the ones we have inside
And then we'll have to hold them there for the last hour of the ride
It's a sign, it's a sign, for an airline of our times
It a sign for an airline of our times
Well they don't make it easy friends
And they don't make it fun
So my brain's been working overtime
And here's what should be done
I'm going to start an airline that will take away the danger
So you won't have to be afraid of an alien or stranger
It's called "U-Naked Airlines" and we'll fly you in the buff
It may sound weird, but you'll have no fear that you won't be safe enough
It's a sign, it's a sign, for an airline of our times
It a sign for an airline of our times
When you get to "U-Naked" take your clothes off, then you'll lie
Upon a warm conveyer belt for a thorough MRI
No carry-ons, explosives, no plastique, no TNT
You are the bare essentials, safe for you and good for me
It's a sign, it's a sign, for an airline of our times
It a sign for an airline of our times
We just made it easy friends
And it just might be fun
Fly "U-Naked"....you'll rest easy on your buns
(spoken)...As you board we'll ask you to step to the rear...and please, no tailgating.

The issue is slightly less serious in nature than the atom bomb, but it affects all of us. We know the need for security, but we can also relax a bit by poking a bit of fun. This sort of humor appeals to audiences because it is neither silly nor totally serious, but something we can all relate to.

Parody differs from satire in that it relies on imitation of a person or genre. It is impossible to list the number song parodies (have fun someday doing a parody search on YouTube) that have been created over the centuries, but the popularity of the medium is telling. Sometimes the parodist is making fun of the song and its artist and even emulates the style of the performer. A less obvious, but still effective, type of parody is the use of a well-known song and the general theme it projects, as a basis for a songwriter's own point.

Some contemporary songs are just ripe for parody. One of these is *Sixteen Tons,* written by Merle Travis and made popular by Tennessee Ernie Ford. The fact that it has been used in parody extensively shows its brilliance. A quick search on parodies of this song revealed political commentary such as "Sixteen Yuan" (Apple computers in China), but also many generally pointless versions about subjects ranging from indigestion (Sixteen Tums), to a woman's excessive weight. These latter serve no purpose and are more "lampoon" than they are satire.

True social parody has a worthy topic and emulates both the original tone and construction of the original. Plato felt that humor was a mixture of pleasure and pain, and psychological studies reveal that we humans find comedy in tragedy, which helps us cope with stress. How often do we laugh at the misfortune of another (the old "slipping on a banana peel" joke) even while sympathizing?

It is in this sense that humor provides "pathos", allowing the artist to communicate to the audience in a special way. To do this well, we need to find the right "sweet spot". Humor can fail miserably depending on our understanding of the audience. The right psychological distance is needed to keep from offending people while still making a point.

To illustrate parody used in ways that illustrate a point while not being offensive or threatening, let's look at two parodies of Sixteen Tons: *Sixteen Holes* by John Denver, and *Four Years of College* by Ben Grosscup.

Guest Artist: Ben Grosscup

Ben Grosscup, a social activist from Amherst, Massachusetts performs songs of struggle and social critique, taking on issues like student debt and other economic problems.

Ben has a B.A. in Anthropology of Science and Technology from Hampshire College, focusing on questions of democracy and technology. He currently works as a community organizer with the Northeast Organic Farming Association/ Massachusetts Chapter. Based in Western Massachusetts, he serves on the board of the ISE.

Ben is an alumnus of the Institute for Social Ecology where he studied from 2001-2003. During that time, he also interned as a community organizer with the ISE Biotechnology Project. He was the organizer the 2005 Social Ecology Intensive Colloquium, and has been organizing the annual Social Ecology Colloquiums regularly since 2007. Grosscup has been organizing the Massachusetts Town-to-Town Campaign on genetic engineering, and he is an elected member of Amherst Town Meeting, which has passed the Bring the War Dollars Home Resolution in 2011.

One hot topic today is student debt. Our education system has exploded to the point that in order to get a college education, students have mortgaged their early years.

In "Four Years of College", co-written with Fred Wulcan, Ben uses parody for the purpose of shedding light on the issue of student debt. To achieve success with the parody, Ben has to understand his audience.

Four Years Of College by Ben Grosscup © 2008

Some people say you gotta get a degree
And after four years, you have to pay back the fees.
Now I'm paying my fees, out on my own
How'm I ever gonna pay back my student loans?
    Chorus: You go four years of college, and what do you get?
    Another diploma and a mountain of debt.
    Saint Peter, don't you call me, 'cause I must stay –
I owe my soul to Sallie Mae.
I borrowed for school so I could get smart,
I studied my books and I did my part.
I took a full load of English and biology,
And then I got a job serving coffee and tea.
    Chorus
The collector kept callin', and he taunted and lied,
But I couldn't pay no matter how much I tried.
I owed so much, it felt like a joke
To pay back my loans I'd forever be broke.
    Chorus
Now they garnish my wages, and the courts decree
The debt follows you even after bankruptcy
Who will carry my burden when I'm dead and gone?
For my student debt will still live on.
    Chorus
Dreams can wither from neglect and delay
Working jobs that you hate for a debt you can't pay
But if everyone whose worn the cap and gown
Stopped paying our debt, we'd take Sallie Mae down!

Then for four years of college, what could you get
besides all that knowledge that you'll forget?
How 'bout a better world for you and for me?
Where higher education's universal and free.
Where higher education is universal and free.

Audience: Grosscup is sure that the audience must be familiar with the song he uses for his melody, in this case, *Sixteen Tons.* The tune and the concept make a great base for his getting his point across. The other reference that the audience must "get" in order to understand the song is the reference to Sallie Mae. This corporation was the original "Student Loan Marketing Association" and had a federal charter for providing federal student education loans. The company has gone public and no longer has a charter, but is still the biggest dealer in the student loan market. The name is recognizable to Ben's audience and makes the perfect reference.

Purpose: *Sixteen Tons* also makes a great canvas John Denver's parody of golf called *Eighteen Holes.*[3] Both songs are humorous. The difference between the two is in purpose. Denver is having fun and his main aim is to be entertaining. Ben intends for his song to be entertaining as well, but also enlightening – to provide a rally call for changes in the system.

Both purposes need to follow some rules of parody, which often means to ridicule. However, parody is used a little differently when used in music. This concept originated as a classical music term in which there is a reworking of one kind of composition into another. There was nothing satirical about it; however, that use has changed over time and implies humor and satire where the familiar becomes the base for a different, and often incongruous, meaning.

It isn't enough to simply put new words to someone else's tune. The parody in the case of Denver and Grosscup's songs is in the mimicking of the song's meaning in a different context. To achieve this, these parody authors have adapted their subject matter. In both cases, a difficult task has been likened to the coal mining subject matter of the original song.

Each author has chosen particular phrases and imagery that best suits his purpose. The titles mimic the original: "Eighteen Holes" and "Four Years" and the choruses stay true to the original in construction and reference:

Denver:
You play eighteen holes, what do you get
Another day older and deeper in debt
Saint Andrew don't you call me, 'cause I can't go
I owe my soul to the country club pro.

Grosscup:
You go four years of college, and what do you get?
Another diploma and a mountain of debt.
Saint Peter, don't you call me, 'cause I must stay –
I owe my soul to Sallie Mae.

Original:
You load sixteen tons, what do you get?
Another day older and deeper in debt.
Saint Peter don't you call me 'cause I can't go
I owe my soul to the company store.

Topic: After that, each author uses references that best illustrate his topic and purpose. The connection has been made and the audience is with them. For the parody to be effective, however, it should have some connection with the original theme as well. Now, likening golf to coal mining might seem a stretch, and a very ironic one, since the coal miner in the original song was unlikely to have ever stepped on a golf course. That is what makes the song humorous however, and there is many of golfer who knows exactly what John is talking about – a game of golf can seem like a day in a coal mine sometimes.

In Grosscup's song, the point of overwhelming student debt is one that his audience will be familiar with because it is a hot topic today. Is being loaded down with debt after undergoing the rigors of a college education as tough as working in a coalmine and only being allowed to buy from the overpriced company store? Of course not. But we don't care – the point is made and the comparison between the coal company and the mortgage banker is an apt one. The use of parody helps illustrate that.

Style: Both parodists mimic the rhyme scheme: AA/BB. Denver chooses to start his song with a phrase taken directly from the original:

Denver:
When you see me tee up, you'd better step aside,
A lot of men didn't, a lotta men died.

Original:
If you see me comin', better step aside,
A lotta men didn't, a lotta men died.

In the case of his topic, this works well. Because his parody is for entertainment reasons, Denver has leeway with his topic. His parody is in structure only and not in purpose.

Grosscup's version is more in keeping with the general substance of the original song than is Denver's. He uses enough lyrical references to make the parody work. Throughout the song you can hear the lyrical references:

> *Some people say/ four years . . . and what do you get/*
> *Saint Peter, don't you call me, 'cause I must stay –*
> *I owe my soul to Sallie Mae.*

We definitely get it. This allows Ben to ensure that the audience understands his comparison of the debts that are incurred in both songs. The parody format works for both Denver and Grosscup, allowing them to use pathos to connect with their audience; meanwhile they illustrate the effectiveness of explaining the unfamiliar by using something familiar, and of the use of different technique depending on purpose.

PREACHING TO THE CHOIR

One additional thing to take into consideration when analyzing how to approach our audience is our attitude toward them. What do they already know? What do they need to know? What do they value?

We can't always know all of these things, but when we sing to those in our own communities sometimes we find it easy to "preach to the choir." There are times doing this is appropriate. For instance, your purpose may be to write a sing-along for an anti-war rally or a themed song for a particular occasion populated by those whose attitudes parallel yours. This is a special talent that, while not intended to persuade as such, still requires an understanding of purpose and audience.

For instance, after a major mass shooting involving assault rifles, you might be asked to lead a rally calling for their ban; however, you might also be asked to lead a vigil for those who had died. In both cases, you might want to come up with a musical phrase that everyone can sing with you; however, in one case, "band together to ban the guns," might be the right approach, while another may require something more general, aimed at healing like "pray for peace".

Logic is often used in these types of songs, however, it is common for the writer to use a modified form of logic that was discussed earlier, the enthymeme. This type of argument is built on common assumptions of the target audience.

Two highly different songs about immigration are Ray Stevens' *Come to The USA* and Neil Diamond's *America*. They differ widely based on audience and purpose, but both depend on the use of truncated logic (enthymeme). *Come to the USA* portrays the USA as a welcoming haven for immigrants by comparing it to countries like China, South Korea, and Iraq, (commonly held general knowledge that is mostly accurate.) Then Stevens plays to many people's belief that when immigrants get here they get free stuff, (some truth, but exaggerated) and are actually encouraged to commit crimes like prostitution. Without actually drawing a conclusion, he is attempting to convince his audience, with their own assumptions, that immigrants come to America only for economic profit.

On the other hand, Neil Diamond appeals to those more lofty assumptions that most of us have about immigration. People come to "freedom's light burning warm" and to realize their "dream". He invokes a passage from that famous song *America the Beautiful*. The assumption here is that his audience agrees that immigrants come for freedom. The first song appeals to our worst instincts, while the second song appeals to our best.

Both songs have a purpose and an intended audience that will draw its own conclusions. Songs like this don't usually convince the opposition, but rather those who agree to their premises are drawn to them.

But the more challenging purpose is to expose listeners to views they have not thought about, or even more challenging, to cause them to change their views about a topic. As we craft our songs of purpose, we need to keep our audience's needs in mind. Choosing the approaches via **Ethos**, **Pathos**, or **Logos** should be a conscious effort.

PART IV: GENTLE PERSUASION

Thaw, with her gentle persuasion, is more powerful than Thor with his hammer. The one melts, the other breaks into pieces.

~ Henry David Thoreau

There is one kind of songwriting that is always for a purpose: social activism. Those who focus on songwriting to create change are always focused on purpose. That doesn't mean that they don't sometimes allow themselves to write for the reason that they would like to vent about an issue they are passionate about. We sometimes have no purpose or audience in mind – we just have a reason. However, often the purpose follows the reason.

But what is "social activism"? According to Amherst College "social activism is an intentional action with the goal of bringing about social change" (www.amherst.edu).

Ah. Intentional. Just like our songwriters with a purpose. Social – well, that's the people who make up society. Change – to make something different. That difference can occur in many ways.

Social activism is usually thought of in political terms. Activists are loud. Activists march, and picket, and canvas. But not everyone who cares about a cause has the time and energy for what amounts to pushing a rock uphill. There is a new breed of activism known as "quiet activism". Sometimes activism is a group of people without a leader or organizational structure and other times it is one person living his/her conscience.

If by simply being, by living your life proudly in the face of adversity, you are being socially active. If you support others, by donating, by cheering them on as audience, you are being social active.

As a songwriter, if you challenge people to think in a new way you are causing social change. Great changes often begin with baby steps. The seed must be planted and sometimes that is the best way.

Activist songwriters approach their purpose in different ways. There is no one "right way." All you need to be an activist is to change society, even if that change is as small as getting one person to think.

Anthems are great, (think *We Shall Overcome*) and have had, and will continue to have, their place in American social movements. Sometimes there is no other way than saying something is wrong and has to be changed. Very often our purpose as writers is to take a stand, with no quibbling. In her very famous song about unions, *Which Side Are You On,* Florence Reece says "there are no neutrals here," and asks "will you be a lousy scab or will you be a man?" There is no reconciliatory tone in this song – she has a point to make.

If you know your beliefs soundly, if your purpose is to let the world know those beliefs, then go ahead with a straightforward activist approach. Do not worry that there are those who might never hear you – many will.

However, there are times when a diplomatic approach is necessary, as it makes even stubborn people think and perhaps come around to our way of thinking.

Example: Bill Steele's song *Garbage* uses a lot very visual examples in the life of Mr. Thompson in order to quietly imprint the impact of our everyday impact on the environment in people's minds:

Mr. Thompson calls the waiter and he orders steak and 'taters
And he leaves the bone and gristle and he never eats the skin.
The bus boy comes and takes it, with a cough contaminates it,
And he throws it in a can with coffee grounds and tuna tins.
Then a truck comes by on Friday and it hauls it all away
And a thousand more just like it hit the landfill everyday.

His chorus then asks the question, "What will we do when there is no place left to put all the garbage?"

Tish Hinojosa uses narrative and pathos to call attention to the plight of the immigrant farm worker in her song, *Something in the Rain.* Her narrator is a young immigrant boy who relates the story of his family as they work the fields. He provides us with a poignant picture of their lives:

When trouble comes our way/ I've seen my daddy pray.

But the real "purpose" of the song creeps up on us. His little sister had something wrong with her that made his mama shake and hold her, and then she goes away. Then we are told there is "something in the rain" and the airplanes "cure the plants" and the environmental statement becomes clear. Finally, she hits hard at the end of the song in order to encourage activism to change the system. We must "change the system" and "change the hurting fields". It is not enough to "talk" and "dream" and we are left with the desire to break through the "sins of man who's profits rape the land" and "break the killing chains".

This is a thoughtful song that requires much of the listener, but the impact is profound for those who take the time to do so.

Turning Reason into Purpose:

When trying to take our reason and focus on our purpose, the tenets of good writing composition and rhetoric become very helpful.

Certainly pathos is important. Making the audience "feel" the pain of others is one way to get it to respond and act in a positive way.

Logic (**Logos**) is more difficult, but being able to state a reasonable premise or list a variety of reasons from which to draw a conclusion is a very important technique by which to convince your audience to change its mind or at least think about your cause.

However, the most difficult aspect, I believe, is **Ethos**. To really bring a tough audience along, those that don't have any great affinity for our songs, ourselves, or our messages requires an additional skill – the ability to see the "other side".

Previously, I mentioned the tendency activists have for "preaching to the choir". It is not always easy to do that well (it requires succinct lyrical phrases and repetition) but it is easier than using appeals. We can write songs with very definite messages that contain "black and white" appeals, and we can sing anthems easily when we know our audience "gets us." It is much harder to appeal to the audience that is not in the choir. Heck, some of them can't even carry the tune.

Many activist writers have decided to not worry about that other side. They feel that their message is the right one and needs to be heard. They have the strength and confidence to write the hard hitting messages whether or not their audiences sing along, whether or not they are entertaining, whether or not they are received well. And throughout long careers of activist songwriting, they achieve great things.

But for many folks, this approach is daunting. Some would rather take a softer approach. This approach requires another part of the persuasive mode that requires "seeing the other side." This doesn't mean that the songwriter has to outline what the opposing views are, it simply means that the tone of the song indicates that the singer realizes there are other views out there and that the people holding those views are not bad people. Meanwhile, the songs hold fast to the principles that the songwriter espouses.

Sometimes issues are very polarizing; it seems impossible to make a point when conflict seems the only scenario. However, as long as you can project real contact and accountability, you can often at least make people think about your point of view without alienating them.

Songwriters who can "see the other side" often have trouble writing songs of social activism. It becomes too hard. There are too many grey areas.

The following quote is attributed to F. Scott Fitzgerald: "The test of first-rate intelligence is the ability to hold two opposed ideas in mind at the same time and still retain the ability to function." This remark illustrates the reason why we often find it so important to just choose a side and go with it – seeing both sides requires a great amount of work!

However, the idea seems to have originated with Aristotle: "It is the mark of an educated mind to be able to entertain a thought without accepting it." I like the philosophy espoused here. The "educated" person learns all that he/she can about a topic. They "entertain" all possibilities. Then, they decide what accept.

This quote makes me feel better when I sit and ponder a way to get my point across when I really do understand the point of view I am opposing. No matter how compelling two sides of an argument may be, we eventually must arrive at a conclusion.

I guess that is why my socially conscious songs tend to lean on narrative. Letting my voice simply tell the story of a real person removes me from the equation and lets the audience make up its own mind. Not hitting too hard, but telling an evocative story, keeps my audience with me so that perhaps they will hear the message. (One song I have written that always catches the audience is *Before The Fire*, which I discuss later. Yes, it is history, but it also asks us to see how our racial issues today were set in place previously. I don't say that in so many words, but allow the audience to have something to think about.)

If you "understand" something in only one way, then you scarcely understand it at all, because when you get stuck, you'll have nowhere to go. But if you represent something in several ways, then when you get frustrated enough, you can switch among different points of view, until you find one that works for you! That is where knowledge of the rhetorical triangle and the rhetorical appeals is helpful. Sometimes we need to focus on creating "**more ethos**".

More Ethos

So how do we go about "seeing the other side"? Well, sometimes we just have to go as far as "establishing common ground". This is the basis of what is known as Rogerian argument, based on the philosophies of humanist, Carl Rogers. Rogerian argument is a conflict-solving technique based on finding similarities of opinion instead of engaging in polarizing debate. This too, can be considered social activism because it is capable of causing change and in making society aware.

Sometimes our purpose in songwriting is not to "win over" someone on a topic but rather to establish common ground with our listeners, hopefully get them thinking, and perhaps at least reach a compromise.

We can achieve this simply by acknowledging that we are part of the problem. In his song *Change Myself*, Todd Rundgren says:

"How can I change the world when I can't change myself?" The song is a great example for Rogerian argument as he reminds us:

Both of us want to win this fight
Both of us think the other is mistaken, so mistaken
Meanwhile, everyone wants to take up sides
So everyone helps us to fall apart

Michael Jackson is looking at the *Man in the Mirror* to ask for change.

I'm starting with the man in the mirror
I'm asking him to change his ways
And no message could have been any clearer
If you wanna make the world a better place
Take a look at yourself, and then make a change

Compromise can be as simple as just asking the question, as Cat Stevens did in *Peace Train*:

I've been crying lately
Thinking about the world as it is
Why must we go on hating?
Why can't we live in bliss?

The use of "we" puts everyone in the same camp.

In *Lost Woman*, Ani Difranco paints a vivid picture to reveal the plight of a woman seeking abortion. She never lets go of her assertion in the right to choose, but the speaker reminds us of reality – anger sometimes isn't enough. In the end, she states the simple truth: "I don't think there is one of us leads a life free of mistakes." Will this get to the most die-hard of anti-abortionists who "keep pounding their fists on reality hoping it will break." No, but it may resonate with those who think and who believe, as it says in the Christian scripture, to let any of you who is without sin, cast the first stone.

Songs are not thesis papers. There isn't time enough to state all the pros and cons of an issue. But sometimes you can sneak in a reference that shows that you know the issue is multi-faceted. This does not mean that you let go of your belief, but only that you show understanding of another point of view. However, only do so if you truly have that understanding. An audience can sometimes sense when it is being pandered to. Honesty is also important.

The songwriter who is a quiet activist is just as important to social change as the one who is able to lead marches and get those hard-hitting ideas out there. If through your songs you plant that seed that eventually grows into a belief to better this world, you are a social activist.

If you know your beliefs soundly, if your purpose is to let the world know those beliefs, then go ahead with a straight-forward activist approach. There are those who will never hear you, but that might be the case no matter what. Again, it all depends on what you are trying to achieve and requires an understanding of your audience.

PART V: THE MODES OF DEVELOPMENT

It's not the name of the tool; it's how you use it.

For rhetoric, he could not ope
His mouth, but out there flew a trope;
And when he happen'd to break off
I' th' middle of his speech, or cough,
H' had hard words, ready to show why,
And tell what rules he did it by;
Else, when with greatest art he spoke,
You'd think he talk'd like other folk,
For all a rhetorician's rules
Teach nothing but to name his tools.
Samuel Butler,
Hudibras, Part I (1663–1664), Canto I, line 81

The rhetorical modes are not an end into themselves, and while it is nice to be able to name your tools, it is much better to have an understanding of when they are effective.

The idea for classifying discourse into categories may have originated from the Greeks as well, (classically know as "topoi"), but Robert Connors in his *The Rise and Fall of the Modes of Discourse* locates what he believes to be their beginnings in an 1827 text by Samuel Newman. These categories eventually found their way into the majority of college textbooks by the 1950's.

An ex-professor of mine, Frank D'Angelo, felt that the modes arose from the "recognition that writers do indeed describe, they sometimes narrate, they do sometimes explain, and they do sometimes hope to persuade" (*A Conceptual Theory of Rhetoric*). It would seem to be very organic. I will leave it to the scholars to debate this. However, the important thing to remember is that these are a few tools to draw from that have been used for centuries in the art of communication and can be very helpful to the songwriter.

Originally there were four basic modes:

Narration
Description
Persuasion
Exposition (Latin for 'showing forth')

We get help in exposition through illustration, cause and effect, classification and division, comparison, process analysis, and definition—these modes are crucial to helping writers explain.

Narration

"Stories make us more alive, more human, more courageous, more loving."

~ Madeleine L'Engle

Simply put, to narrate is to tell a story. The desire to listen to and create stories is basic to the human condition. Our stories suit our purpose and we use them to shed light on the human condition and provide illustrations of the point we wish to make.

The prime directive of story telling is "show don't tell." This only means that typically a good story song will make its point through details and attention to the rhetorical triangle. The audience will then understand without being told.

Topic: To write a good narrative your must you must first have a solid main idea. This might take some brainstorming and editing until you have gotten rid of the myriad of things that surround your idea. Writing good narrative means selecting good details. Only the details that advance the point should be used. A definite sequence of events is also very important. How are the details unfolding? Is the story told in a chronological way or will you use a technique like flashback or flashforward?

Speaker: All narrative must have a narrator. Who is speaking? Is it you, the singer? There are only a few "points of view" and they are known as first person (I) second person (you) third person (he, she, it) and omniscient (the narrator knows everything but doesn't need a pronoun). Point of view is immensely important as it conveys our ethos and provides the believability necessary to get the point across. Stories also have a "tense" – is the story in the past, present or future? Once established, it is important to keep the point of view and tense consistent.

Audience: While it is sometimes difficult to gauge who our audience will be (some "impetus" situations allow us to know the extent of understand our audience will have. However, we often do not now who will be listening to our song. Therefore, we must choose the details that help audiences understand our point and that can mean choosing details that further understanding, making the story easy to follow.

Stories can be fact or fiction, or a combination of both. (See the section on Illustration for more on this.) Good stories have a plot, characters, and a beginning and an end. They often have friction of some kind, and then a resolution. The history of song is filled with songs that tell stories in with a plot and a solid conclusion. In the song *The Night The Lights Went Out in Georgia,* there is a well-defined plot with named characters and a surprise conclusion when we find out it is "little sister" who aimed her gun.

Important aspects of narrative

Tone
Point of View
Choice of Details
Organization
Verb Tense

Tone is essential to conveying meaning. During your writing, you are conveying an emotional state that is important to your purpose. You might intend to convey sadness or anger. Perhaps the tone is conciliatory, kind, or encouraging. To do this as songwriters, we pay particular attention to our word choice.

There are two ways to define words: Denotation and Connotation. Words do have very neutral, dictionary meanings. You can go straight to dictionary.com and find that sort of definition. But perhaps more important to the message in purposeful writing is what is known as the connotation. The connotation of a word holds emotional associations. Some of these are obvious. The word "crippled" has a negative connotation, while "handicapped" has a more positive one. "Slim" is a lot more appealing that "skinny". "Economical" is something to aspire to, while "stingy" is best to be avoided. When choosing words, we need to keep our audience in mind. Use your words wisely or risk losing goodwill or impeding meaning. Language affects narrative greatly. For instance, it is very important when conveying **pathos**, to use the right word. Is a suicide bomber called a "terrorist" or a "martyr"? Is there a "problem" in your city, or is it a "cancer"?

This kind of narrative occurs in Paul Simon's *America*. The narrator is not named but his companion is Cathy. Otherwise we know nothing about them. This song includes several narrative moments and the "tone" or feeling of being lost, of searching, pervades the song. There is an overall theme of searching juxtaposed with the exuberance of youth and the perpetual desire of those who are looking for America. People understand, when they hear this narrative, that the plot is not the purpose and cannot help but be touched by the sense of ambiguity and longing.

Point of View

Performing songwriters bear an extra burden over non-performing writers. Because we are the ones up there singing, it is assumed that everything we write is about ourselves. That is often the case, of course. However, many songwriters wish to focus on a purpose that is beyond a personal story or feeling. This sense of purpose allows for writing the song in something other than the first person. Every song does not have to have an "I", "we", or a "me" in it. There are millions of these, and they are usually written to express a personal feeling. Sometimes the first person is the correct choice, because it adds ethos.

Sometimes, it is more effective to write the song using the third person (he, she, it). However, it is still important to the listener who automatically assumes the singer knows the person of whom they are speaking. And sometimes they might. For example, after his very public breakup with Miranda Lambert, it isn't a stretch to see the personal when Blake Shelton sings (a song he didn't write), *She's Got A Way With Words*, and he doesn't fight the assumption.

Then, there is the third person omniscient viewpoint (all-seeing and Godlike with the ability to see inside anyone's head.

An example of this viewpoint is *Eleanor Rigby,* (Lennon-McCartney). Or we might use the passive voice (no narrator is identified, rather the action is "being done" but the actor is unknown.) In *We Weren't Born to Follow,* Bon Jovi sings 'This road was paved by the hopeless and the hungry" using passive voice throughout the verse, but switching to third person in the chorus.

Another point of view is first person, but in the guise of another. This technique is known as "personae". In this case, the singer becomes an actor, and while the song is in the first person the audience quickly knows that the narrator is not the singer. Singer/Songwriter Mark Stepakoff uses this technique to his advantage in his award-winning narrative song, *Cold Blood,* which will be discussed later in the chapter.

One can never assume anything about how the audience hears us. Even the best-laid plans go awry. Once, after I sang, "My name is Fannie Taylor and in 1923 . . . (*Before The Fire*), an audience member approached me and said in an embarrassed fashion, "I hate to ask, but did that really happen to you?" (In text speak: LOL!) I give her the benefit of the doubt – it was the first line of the song after all, and maybe she hadn't quite honed in yet. This is example of an anomaly, of course, but it is an illustration of how hard it can be to make an audience really hear everything.

Details

A good story has to have the right selection of details in order to guarantee that the listener will follow the story. It is important to make sure that all of the details chosen are relevant to the main point of the story. Remember, a good popular song is probably between 2 ½ to 4 minutes long. There isn't time for a lot of digression and every detail matters. You want details that move the plot forward and help your audience see and feel what is happening. Anything else is just distracting. Songs like *Ode to Billie Joe* and *Desperados Waiting For a Train* include specific details that paint a scene or move a plot along. I read that being a journalistic writer makes things easy. You can just read a story of someone's life and then all you have to do is put it into meter and rhyme. I can't say I agree with that in all cases, especially when the song has a purpose beyond simply relating the sequence of events. Yes, the information is there for you. You don't have to depend on your imagination, but there are so many choices to make. Which details to select are among those choices and that can make all of the difference to your audience's understanding of your topic and is especially important when you have a purpose.

Organization

The order in which we tell our story is also very important, and there is more than one way to organize a narrative. One obvious way is strictly chronological: first this happened, then that happened etc. However, there are other options. One can use the "flashback" technique of starting in the future and then going backward to explain how you got there. In the song, *Honey* recorded by Bobby Goldsboro, we start with "tree how big it's grown" and go back to when it wasn't big. There is often a "twist" (*The Nights the Lights Went Out in Georgia*) or surprise during this type of organization. It is also possible to write in "reverse chronological order" and work from the ending back to the beginning such as occurs in the country classic, *Long Black Veil.* It is important for your story clarity to organize your details in a consistent manner. Is it a simple story from beginning to end? Does the story arc to a tension that is resolved? Do you want to keep the listener on the edge of their seats by starting at the present, intriguing the audience, and then telling them what happened to arrive there?

Verb Tense

Finally, it is important to watch the tenses of your verbs when writing stories. Make it clear if things are happening in the past, present, or future. Look carefully at your verbs and make sure that the time of the action is where you want it to be. Tenses can be combined in stories, depending on the organizational structure.

Guest Artist:
Mark Stepakoff

Mark is an award winning songwriter and performer in the Boston area. He is an eleven-time winner for the *American Songwriter Magazine* including 1st Prize (twice), 2nd Prize, and "lyric spotlight" feature. Other awards include the USA Songwriting Competition (seven time winner), the Great American Songwriting Contest (Three-time 1st Prize winner, six other times named top 5 winner, twelve other times selected as Finalist, three Honors Awards. He was the only songwriter to ever receive 1st Prize in consecutive years. Mark was named to the contest's "Songwriters' Hall of Fame"). He has also won awards in the John Lennon Songwriting Competition—the list goes on.

His song "Cold Blood" won first place in *American Songwriter,* the Great American Song Contest and has placed in many more.

You can find out more about Mark and listen to his music at www.markstepakoff.com

Cold Blood © Mark Stepakoff 2013

She said she saw my ad in the telephone book
Her sink it was leaking; could I take a look?
She gave me her address and I wrote it down
Then I drove my truck over to the rich part of town
I walked up the drive from the quiet cul-de-sac
I heard a voice tell me to come round the back
She stood in the shadows and beckoned me in
That's when I saw the bruises just under her chin

And cold blood ran through my veins
Cold as the storms on the Alberta plains
That many a time cause the rivers to flood
Yes I felt the rushing of cold blood

Guess she needed someone in whom to confide
So she opened the door, and she showed me inside
We sat in the kitchen; she poured us some tea
I could smell her perfume as she sat down next to me
Her husband, she said, owned the Second Street Bank
And his temper was bad and was worse when he drank
Which she said pretty much every day was the case
Then he'd come home at night and put a fist to her face

And cold blood ran through my veins
Cold as the hail through the Iowa rains
That can cause a spring crop to be nipped in the bud
Yes my heart was pumping out cold blood

It was seven long years since I'd been in the hole
Yeah but technically I was still on parole
So I wasn't supposed to be packing a gun
Oh but you can be sure I knew how to get one
The very next morning, as you might have read

I stormed into the bank, and put the gun to his head
He pleaded and begged me to spare him his life
Saying "Don't hurt me Mister, I've got a young wife"
And cold blood ran through my veins
Cold as the pistol I held to his brains
Then I watched as he fell with a sickening thud
Yes I shot that bastard in cold blood

The newspapers called it a botched robbery
A crazy ex-con on a murderous spree
With no explanation for his evil ways
And a young widow left now to mourn all her days
My sentence was long, but my trial it was short
She sat the whole time in the back of the court
No show of emotion, no words did she say
But her eyes looked at mine as they took me away

And cold blood ran through my veins
Cold as the iron on these shackles and chains
That I'll wear till I'm laid 'neath the earth and the mud
And my body's been drained of its cold blood

Meanwhile far away in the rich part of town
She pours a martini and lets her hair down
It goes down so easy, that Tanqueray gin
As easy as painting a bruise on her chin
The truth is her husband was kind and sincere
He loved her to pieces; he bored her to tears
She longed for his money and bided her time
I guess that her blood's even colder than mine

Yes cold blood runs through her veins
On her mantle's a vase with her husband's remains
While she's sleeping tonight with some handsome young stud
Well her flesh may be warm, but she's got cold blood

Let's look at the development of the story. This song is a true narrative, in that it is all 'story' from beginning to end. It has characters. It has a theme. It has a plot. It has a beginning and an end.

This is a first person narrative. However, the "I" in the story is not Mark Stepakoff, but rather he sings in the "persona" of someone else. We don't know this person's name, nor the name of the "she" in the story. Names are unimportant. Through details, Mark quickly lets us know who these people are. The speaker is a plumber. We know that immediately. A couple of stanzas later, we know he is an ex-con on parole. We also know he is quick tempered, as just a glimpse of that bruise causes anger. We don't know much about the woman, but early in the song we know she was rich, wore perfume, and later she is described as "young". Oh, and she has bruises under her chin. Thus begins the plot.

The story begins immediately with the action and we quickly get to the point. The wife has been abused, so she says. The action continues quickly with the man getting a gun, killing the husband, going to trial, gets convicted, while she quietly watches.

The details and chronology are chosen well and we get a visual picture of the locations and never lose track of what is happening. Mark uses great descriptive detail to propel the story, and also makes sure that it stays in the past tense – it is important to keep tense consistent when writing a narrative. The sequence of events is clear, as it should be in a good story, and we are never lost.

The story is told in the past tense but in strict chronology, switching to the present tense only at the end – the place where the speaker is relating this story. This type of structure allows the story to relate the "twist": that the woman used the plumber to get rid of her husband. Stepakoff stays in the past tense until the second to last chorus, where he switches to the present and stays there for one more verse and a last chorus.

One key to the success of this story, which might seem to have "been done before", is that Mark uses language to make it his own. There is the use of the words "cold blood" in several different ways. First we see the cold blood that is the speaker's as he focuses first on the abusive husband. Later the description is used to describe his feelings towards the deceptive woman. He is finally drained of his cold blood and will be buried with it. In the end, it is her cold blood that he contrasts to her warm flesh.

In an interview with *American Songwriter Magazine*, Mark comments on the importance of words in this song: "I have two lines tied as my favorites, 'Yes, I shot that bastard in cold blood,' and, 'As easy as painting a bruise on her chin.' Both lines are a significant development in the story. 'Yes I shot that bastard in cold blood' is the murder of the story, and it's the perfect example of the tone I wanted for the "gun-for-hire" protagonist who tells the story. 'As easy as painting a bruise on her chin' is the line that reveals the twist of the story – the femme fatale used the narrator to kill her husband so that she could take his money."

The purpose of this story is simply to entertain. "I had the murder ballad idea in mind," Mark said, "but I didn't really know where I was going at first. I liked the femme fatale and the idea of a protagonist with a dark past. So, I had to start with an idea and just see where it would take me. The process was probably close to a month of writing. I wrote a little everyday. I just needed three or four good lines a day to advance the plot and there was also a lot of revision. I went through several drafts. The most difficult part for me is writing a good story and also making sure it's a good song. It's easy for details of a story not to matter. You have to focus a listener completely on the story for it to be a successful song. You have to make sure every line advances the story or plot in some way."

In the case of "Cold Blood", Mark's impetus was a desire to write a murder ballad. His purpose was simply to make a good story that was clear to his audience. The narrative form gets our attention, and you can see how well it can be used for a song where the meaning is important, especially in the case of songs that might want to advocate for a particular cause.

Northern White by Jane Fallon

I am fond of using the story form, and in my song, *Northern White,* I use a true story to raise awareness about the cause of white sand mining in Wisconsin. The impetus was a song contest that was sponsored by the organization People's Music Network for their "Song of the Month" contest. They wanted songs about hydro-fracking, and being one who likes to look into the sides of issues that might not be obvious, I did some research. In doing so, I stumbled across the situation with what is known as "diamond sand" or what is commonly known as "Northern White."

This sand, I learned, is located only in the northern part of the US and in Southern Canada. It is called "diamond" sand because of its hardness. When coupled with a drill and water, this sand can penetrate shale with greater ease, therefore allowing for easier hydro-fracking.

White sand mining is still a contentious issue in the North. It has brought great prosperity and jobs to small communities, but the age-old question of whether short-term gain outweighs the long-term damage to the land is there.

The story I found was a newspaper article about a woman in Wisconsin. Most of the details are accurate as far as her going to town meeting, confronting the miners, dealing with the townsfolk. As in Mark's song, the characters names are not mentioned. I never mention a real name because that is not important to the message of the song. Nor was there a child involved, however, I felt the third person narrator was most effective. Third person can lend "ethos" while still providing a little objectivity. All the narrator does is relate the events, she doesn't comment on them.

I played with the story's details some. In this case, the feel of the story and the purpose is more important than a simple relating of a newspaper article verbatim. While the particular woman in the article I read did not die of chemicals, I found several links to stories about people whose respiratory health was affected by these chemicals. These "everyman" narratives allow the listener to fill in the blanks themselves. The narrator is non-descript, but the character of the mother is one of pluck. She is willing to stand up to the businessmen and go against others in her community.

The other characters are the businessmen and the community. We see them briefly, but their interaction with the main character is important because their inclusion allows for implementation of those important parts of the rhetorical triangle that gives the topic a purpose. The businessman attempts to appeal to **pathos** (concern for the well-being of the community) when he says, "One six-second weekly blast is all it takes. You might be surprised how little noise we will make." Later, Mama engages in "the other side" **(more ethos)** by assuring her community that she is one of them – she knows it is hard to farm and how tempting this offer is. But then she hits with pure fact **(logos)**: You can't eat gas, you can't drink oil." This is an enthymeme.

> The unspoken **major premise**: We need food and water to live.
> The spoken **minor premise**: We can't eat gas, and we can drink oil."

If people agree to both those premises, then they must draw the conclusion that digging up acres of farmland that might not be able to be replaced in order to frack for gas and oil is not a good thing.

I also made some language decisions that might not be strictly accurate, but which I thought helped in understanding the meaning. To promote the understanding of what is happening, I chose to use the word "hydro-fracker" in the second line and the word "miner" in the fourth. While the white sand people are not technically frackers (they sell to the frackers) I felt it was important that the audience know the connection. Most of the audience would be familiar with hydro-fracking but not as many would know about the white sand issue.

I made the connection with the West Virginia hills myself, because for me the purpose of the song was to show how the earth is connected and to learn from history. Hydro-fracking in

Oklahoma is connected with sand mining in Wisconsin. One has caused the other. In West Virginia we have seen the example of how mountain top removal harmed the landscape and created illness among the miners. This is an attempt at logic on my part:

Premise one: Coal mining has harmed West Virginia.
Premise two: White sand mining is similar to coal mining.
Conclusion: This issue needs attention.

In addition, I attempted to add more pathos in creating the dichotomy of "businessmen "(corporations) in "clean" gray suits whose hands are "dirty" with the northern white. They don't care about the environment, just profits.

You can read the lyrics and see the "purpose" analysis in Part XI, p. 156.

Description

"I am sure," cried Catherine, "I did not mean to say anything wrong; but it is a nice book, and why should I not call it so?"

"Very true," said Henry, "and this is a very nice day, and we are taking a very nice walk; and you are two very nice young ladies. Oh! It is a very nice word indeed! It does for everything."

~ Jane Austen, **Northanger Abbey**, 1803

I am a big Jane Austen fan, and the opening quote indicates why. She was one smart, perceptive writer.

Thesaurus.com lists 45 synonyms for the word "nice" such as friendly, amiable, pleasant, charming, and superior. Dictionary.com provides the categories of the word:

Adjective, nicer, nicest:

1. pleasing; agreeable; delightful: a nice visit.
2. amiably pleasant; kind: They are always nice to strangers.
3. characterized by, showing, or requiring great accuracy, precision, skill, tact, care, or delicacy: nice workmanship; a nice shot; a nice handling of a crisis.
4. showing or indicating very small differences; minutely accurate, as instruments: a job that requires nice measurements.
5. minute, fine, or subtle: a nice distinction.
6. having or showing delicate, accurate perception: a nice sense of color.
7. refined in manners, language, etc.: Nice people wouldn't do such things.

Sometimes when we describe, we fall into a rut. We use words like "nice" because we are too lazy to think of a good substitute. But words have a personality and a specific purpose. Mark Twain said that the difference between the right word and the wrong word is the difference between the lightening and the lightening bug. The well-known Broadway composer, Stephen Sondheim, once said of the Gershwin lyrics to "Summertime" that the word "and" instead of "when" in the opening line was genius.

"That "and" is worth a great deal of attention. I would write "Summertime when" but that "and" sets up a tone, a whole poetic tone, not to mention a whole kind of diction that is going to be used in the play; an informal, uneducated diction and a stream of consciousness, as in many of the songs like My Man's Gone Now. It's the exact right word, and

> *that word is worth its weight in gold. "Summertime when the livin' is easy" is a boring line compared to "Summertime and". The choices of "ands" [and] "buts" become almost traumatic as you are writing a lyric – or should, anyway – because each one weighs so much."*[5]

We have all been schooled in the five senses: touch, taste, sight, sound, and smell. This is how humans relate to their world. There are songs so poetic that the entire song seems filled with the senses and loosely related to a point. Rod McKuen's *Jean* is one of those. The descriptive phrases set a scene and convey a tone, but there is not story line. The purpose is a larger one that is only hinted at: *"you're young and alive, come out of your half-dreamed dream"* and notice this beautiful world. The reason for writing this song was the theme to the movie, *The Prime of Miss Jean Brodie,* and McKuen built on that. However, the underlying purpose is to convey the character of the movie's heroine. If we listen just to the song without knowing anything about the movie, we still get the sense of the woman Jean is, and we ride along on that sensory prose. The descriptive adjectives in the song go from the very common and somewhat mundane (Roses are red, leaves are green) to the metaphorical (hills are ablaze, sun comes a singing) but the general picture emerges of the beauty of the day and of the meadow and the call to wake up to love.

Descriptive words set the mood and establish a tone and are often combined with narration. *Sunday Morning Coming Down* by Kris Kristofferson is filled with sensory images wrapped around a simple moment in time for a down-and-out drifter. In this song, the narrator feels (no way to hold my head that doesn't hurt), touches (fumbles and stumbles) sees (watched a small kid) smells (someone frying chicken) and hears (listen to the songs they were singing). The purpose is wonderfully conveyed through a simple scenario with little plot but instead a narrative vignette with a lot of description. The point of the song is conveyed in the tone that those words create. Kristofferson's description is much more evocative than "I woke up with a hangover on Sunday."

Beware the lonely adjective

In a letter he wrote to a student named D.W. Bowser, Mark Twain said, *"When you catch an adjective, kill it. No, I don't mean utterly, but kill most of them--then the rest will be valuable. They weaken when they are close together. They give strength when they are far apart."* [6] The key to the effectiveness in Kristofferson's song is that it is not all about the adjectives. There is narrative here where description is spread out amid the action. The song isn't just a list of adjectives but there are verbs there as well. The same occurs in *Jean*, if not as concretely. There is action occurring that is combined well with the adjectives, which give the adjectives purpose and strength.

Using descriptive imagery is highly evocative. Our lives are entwined with our senses. Certain smells or sounds take us back to times in our lives. Marcel Proust used this emotion in his epic novel *Membrance of Things Past* when he bites into a madeleine cookie and is transported to a past event.

> *"And soon, mechanically, weary after a dull day with the prospect of a depressing morrow, I raised to my lips a spoonful of the tea in which I had soaked a morsel of the cake. No sooner had the warm liquid, and the crumbs with it touched my palate, a shudder ran through my whole body, and I stopped, intent upon the extraordinary changes that were taking place. An exquisite pleasure had invaded my senses . . . individual, detached, with no suggestion of its origin . . .Whence could it have come to me, this all-powerful joy? I was conscious that it was connected with the taste of tea and cake, but that it infinitely transcended those savours, could not, indeed, be of the same nature as theirs. Whence did it come? What did it signify? How could I seize upon and define it? "* [7]

Songs can use this technique effectively as well. In Stephen Bruton's song *Too Many Memories* (recorded by Patty Loveless and Tom Rush) the narrator says:

There are those moments and they just never fade/
The look in his eyes and the way the light played

Sometimes the memories aren't clear, as in "The Way We Were":

Misty watercolor memories . . . scattered pictures . . . laughter
(Hamlish, Bergman, and Bergman)

However, the descriptive words are still evocative of "the way we were."

John Denver refers to the senses in his song *Annie's Song*, using images and a technique known as simile, in which we use the word "like" to compare something we know in order to explain something we don't know:

You fill up my senses like a night in the forest,
like the mountains in springtime, like a walk in the rain,
like a storm in the desert, like a sleepy blue ocean

(I discuss this technique in further detail when I discuss the comparison mode.)

These images allude to our own feelings of what a night in the forest, etc. might look and feel like, leaving it up to our imaginations to fill in the blanks with our own experience.

Using sensory imagery in song adds to **ethos** – our use of imagery allows the listener to believe we understand our subject matter: it isn't just a "whistle", it's a lonesome one (*Lonesome Whistle*); it isn't a dress, it's that "same old shaggy" one (*Try a Little Tenderness*); it is not just any eyes cryin' in the rain, but "blue" ones. (*Blue Eyes Crying in the Rain*).

An effective way to use description is simply to create what is known as a "dominant impression". In this case, all of the adjectives relate to creating a feeling in the listener, and that feeling (tone) is consistent throughout the song. The "feeling" is never stated, but simply conveyed through the use of language.

One vivid song about racism uses imagery to create a dominant impression by also connecting it to metaphor, which is the use of "one thing for another". (There will be more on this when we discuss comparison). This famous song, *Strange Fruit,* written by a teacher named Abel Meeropol, (published under the name of Lewis Allan) and sung most memorably by Billy Holliday, doesn't waste a word and gets the point across by using very definite sights and sounds which create a haunting dominant impression:

Southern trees bear a strange fruit,
Blood on the leaves and blood at the root,
Black body swinging in the Southern breeze,
Strange fruit hanging from the poplar trees.

--

Here is a fruit for the crows to pluck,
For the rain to gather, for the wind to suck,
For the sun to rot, for a tree to drop,
Here is a strange and bitter crop.

This is a definite example of "show, don't tell" and it is very effective. One cannot read or hear these words without feeling them. The examples above are evidence that songwriters use description for different purposes. When choosing your sensory images, you should focus on your purpose and this overlaps with the other modes of development and rhetorical appeals. What you want to achieve with your song will determine the use of sensory images you need. Your desired objective and knowledge of your audience will determine the number of details you need and how you will use them.

In my song, *Sweet Amazon,* I combine both the narrative and descriptive techniques to both show and tell about dangers to our rain forest.

The narrative is based on a story I read in *Parade Magazine* that discussed the rapid destruction of the rain forest in South America. I used real names (Edimar and Kotok) and the related details such as the 40 miles of destruction are taken from the article. The descriptive words hope to create a visual picture of what is happening: crystal clear streams are becoming brown, but in addition there are a lot of active verbs used for description: deer roam, trees are uprooted, rivulets run, smoke stings. Former ways of living are gone.

The purpose of the song is to remind people that the rain forest is considered the lungs of the world. The destruction of these plants contributes to global warming and affects the air that we breathe.

The logic of the song is an enthymeme. I assume that the audience agrees to the premise that this forest is essential to our life on earth and that current practices can't continue. In addition, there are indigenous tribes whose lives are being ruined.

This provides **pathos**, which catches the readers' ears first. They hone in on the story line coupled with the description. There is **more ethos** in the bridge as it is made clear that yes, we need land for food, but we also need clean air. Because, Brazil and other countries have attempted laws to protect the rain forests, I want to make it clear that it is the "lawless" that continue to impact nature. These are details that the listener might catch on the second or third listen, but it is the narrative, and the description, that will first grab the attention.

<u>Exposition</u>

Exposition simply refers to all the writing that isn't specific to narration, description, or persuasion. The following modes of illustration, cause and effect, classification, and process analysis are those that help us explain.

We discussed that the job of narration and description is to "show don't tell." There is certainly truth in this, especially when it applies to narrative. For instance, let's rewrite Mark Stepakoff's song:

A plumber arrives at the house of a young rich woman. He sees the bruise on her chin and whens she tells him her husband beat her, the plumber, who is an ex-con, gets a gun and shoots the husband. During the trial he realizes that the woman played him for a sucker, drew the bruise on her face, so he gets convicted and sentenced. He imagines her living it up with a new lover as he contemplates his own death.

Song over. Not nearly as much fun is it? The story method is what is essential to that particular song. The details are what set this particular story apart from another that might have a similar plot.

However, when we write in an expository fashion it is important to "tell". We use facts and examples to illustrate our point and get our purpose across. These examples might be narrative or descriptive, but they can also be facts or statistics.

Illustration and Example

Illustrations are examples that support your point. Illustrations can be facts, details, anecdotes, or personal examples. They can be narrative or descriptive. Illustration helps largely in persuasion. Through illustration the writer's position gains validity.

Songs sometimes use one illustration to get their points across, or they may use several. In *Grown Men Don't Cry* by Tom Douglas and Steve Seskin, the singer uses three separate illustrations of times that did make him cry. First he mentions an empathetic situation watching a woman and a child in poverty, secondly a personal story about dream about his father, and finally an uplifting example of his daughter's love. These are three very different illustrations, but all very good examples of what might make a grown man cry.

In *Imagine*, John Lennon gives us several hypothetical examples of what peace would be like. He gives examples of things that divide us and cause friction: religion, nationalism, greed, and hunger. Without these things, perhaps we can learn to live in peace.

In *Black Man*, Stevie Wonder uses a massive list of achievements by people of all colors to prove that we are all one world. It is a history lesson in a song. He gives us 27 historical instances where the black, red, yellow, and white men have made an impact on America to the point to justify his statement that, *"history will repeat again, it's time we learned this World Was Made For All Men."*

Someone asked me about truth. How important is truth when we tell our stories? He wasn't the first to wonder about this:

> *Facts and truth really don't have anything to do with one another.*
>
> ~ William Faulkner
>
> *It is the fault of our rhetoric that we cannot strongly state one fact without seeming to belie some other*
>
> ~ Ralph Waldo Emerson
>
> *"Never let the truth (or facts) stand in the way of a good story".* (This quote has often been attributed to Mark Twain, like so many other sayings, but it actually has a long history going back to the 18th century and has been stated in many languages.)

Mark Twain did say:

> "*If you tell the truth you don't have to remember anything,*"

and

> "*Get your facts first, and then you can distort them as much as you please.*"

I am partial to this last quote when it comes to songwriting. There can be truth in writing that is somewhat like an abstract painting. For instance, the painter Van Gogh began his career largely influenced by the Realism movement, which was the attempt to present objects as they appear. But it also focused the everyday life and Van Gogh eventually went his own way, getting more impressionistic in order to convey this realism. When using details in a song, you choose those details depending on your purpose and audience. If you are hoping to portray a realistic historic event, and your audience knows the details, then be as accurate as possible. If you are hoping to be more metaphorical, or if your purpose doesn't rely on specifics, then use the description needed to get that point across.

Definite facts are sometimes used in songs, but usually confined to dates, times, and historical events. This is where good research comes in. If you want to use a fact in your song, make sure it is correct. Bono, of the band U2, was often reminded that his song *Pride (In the Name of Love)* states that Martin Luther King was shot on April 4th (correct) in the early morning (not correct; he was shot at 6 p.m.). Should it matter? If a detail is in the song for a specific purpose, then it should be correct, especially when it is very specific and easily researched. In this case, the time doesn't really matter to the point of the song, but it can add a distraction that takes a little away from credibility and prevent the song's main message from getting out. Bono would sometimes make a disclaimer on this point before he sang the song from the stage. Having to make this disclaimer just interrupts his very powerful message.

Sometimes a detail missed is not important. There are inaccuracies in Eric Bogle's *The Band Played Waltzing Matilda* (about an Australian soldier who fought at Galipoli during WWI). Among them is a line that states, "They gave me a tin hat". This is anachronistic, as the British and Imperial armies were not issued steel helmets until 1916, the year after Gallipoli. The typical Aussie uniform would have included a cloth "slouch" hat. Die-hard historians might quibble with the accuracy of his description of the landing and battle. However, the rest of the song just breathes authenticity and is filled with so much content that the average listener is not going to hear anything amiss. In fact, "tin" hat is more universal for the global audience. When the lad is handed a tin hat and a gun and sent off to war, the average listener gets immediately what is happening because that would be a more common reference for the larger world.

Robbie Roberts gets it correct in *The Night They Drove Old Dixie Down*:

By May 10th Richmond had fell --
the Danville Train--
Stoneman's Cavalry--
winter of '65.

His purpose, to tell an accurate representation of the end of the war from the loser's perspective, is well served by using accurate details. (Rumor has it that Levon Helm took Robertson to the library when they were at Woodstock so that he could research the history and geography in order to be respectful to the cause.) In this case, the specific facts are essential to creating this song's lasting influence in folk music.

Accuracy is always best when using illustrations, so aspire to that; however, there might be times when your audience might seem to require something less authentic because your particular choice of illustration promotes the meaning and helps achieve the purpose. That is a choice you must make as the writer.

Guest Artist: Mike Glick

Mike Glick is a songwriter based in New York who performs often with his son, Aleksi, in a duo called "Generations." I was doing the beta version of a workshop on this topic at a *People's Music Network* conference and I heard Mike sing this song and asked if I could use it. It seemed to be a fine use of current events as illustration.

On Mike's website at www.generations-music.com, Chris Owens, formerly with NYC's *City Sun* notes, "Mike's treatment of poems and writings by others are respectful and moving. The late Pete Seeger labeled him 'one of the best songwriters going.' Years ago Mike led a quintet with strong USA reviews in The New York Times, Newark Star-Ledger, etc. and overseas (Avante, Lisbon; Odigitis, Athens...)." DJ Nick Noble of WICN-FM Worcester, MA said, "Listeners to my show have commented on the timeliness and effectiveness of *Living While Black,* a powerful part of the folk tradition of social commentary."

Let's take a look at it.

Living While Black – © 2015 words & music Mike Glick

Oh I've rarely been uneasy just walking around
Or felt there was a target on my back
But if your skin makes you step lightly on the ground
Maybe you're living while being Black
And if you're a boy they'll still treat you like a man
But that goes both ways for a fact
And your hoodie's just a mask to the children of the Klan
When you're walking while being Black
It's the unwritten law that's so hard to follow
And ignorance is not an excuse
And if you deny it, your words are just hollow
Talk's just a way to cover the truth
Say you're trying to make a living bending the law
Selling cigarettes out of a pack
Well that's cause for assault; it's your own damn fault
Just try breathing while being Black
So if you're in Walmart holding the wrong toy
Or driving and not "looking right,"
Or offering comfort to your dying boy
There's no way to predict who you'll make uptight
You've got no word that can carry the weight
Of Fox news and all those other hacks
You're the life of the party, but arrived too damn late
Cause you're living while being Black
It's the unwritten law that's so hard to follow
And just keeping that always in mind
Would make me enraged, always stuck on one page
Is that justice, or "just us," who's deaf, dumb and blind?
Oh I've rarely been uneasy just walking around
Or felt there was a target on my back
But if they toss you a life jacket after you've drowned
Maybe you're living while being Black...

Mike's song is a straightforward "cause" song and the illustrations he uses are based on events happening in our society today. His stories relate to real ones and the echo the stories of Freddie Gray, Trayvon Martin, Eric Garner and others. But Glick knows it isn't important to name these individuals. What is more important in a song like this is using enough examples in order to draw the conclusion. This is **inductive logic**.

The examples contain enough real-life descriptions for his contemporary audience will resonate enough. The words "hoodie", "selling cigarettes", "Walmart" will remind people of news stories they have heard and lend realism to the song.

This is an example of a song that is meant to hit hard at the current scene; it has both elements of attempting to change minds via **logic**, but also elements of **preaching to the choir.** His allusion to FOX news will be cheered by a certain demographic, but it might turn another demographic off. However, it makes his intended point that he feels the much of the media is biased.

The song is bookended with the same thought: "I have never had to feel this way". This comes from the speaker. It is evident that the speaker is not black and this establishes a touch of **ethos**. By the very fact that he isn't black, he can be considered more objective as a white person in relating his point. The main concept of these to verses goes back to Wellesley professor Peggy McIntosh's paper called, *White Privilege and Male Privilege: A Personal Account of Coming to See Correspondences Through Work in Women's Studies.*[7] The term "white privilege" has taken off in recent years and you hear it often. Glick refers to that notion, just briefly, by explaining his treatment as a white man.

The song has the same angry feel as Phil Och's *Here's To Mississippi.* Ochs methodically blames the people, the schools, the cops, the judges, the government the laws, and the churches of Mississippi for the injustices of racism. It might not be a song that can be sung for generations in a variety of situations, such as we consider Dylan's *Blowin' in the Wind,* but is a specific song with a specific purpose to relate. Mike Glick's song is an Och's song. He takes a definite stand and, despite the probability that there are those who will argue against him, he makes a very good case for his argument with his list of illustrations.

Division and Classification

Ranking all things under general and special heads renders the nature or uses of a thing more easy to be found out, when we seek in what rank of being it lies.

~Dr. Isaac Watts

Musicians are constantly faced with trying to define our genre. According to guardian.com there are now 1,264 genres of popular music. Take a look at everynoise.com, a website that has created "an ongoing attempt at an algorithmically-generated, readability-adjusted scatter-plot of the musical genre-space". They claim 1,491 genres are used by Spotify. Whenever I post a new CD on cdbaby.com and attempt to call it "folk" I have to decide if I am "like Joni", or perhaps "like Ani". That is unless I am Folk Blues, Folk Jazz, Folk Pop, Folk Rock, Free Folk, Gentle Folk, Traditional Folk or Jazzy Folk. CDbaby (www.cdbaby.com) lists 45 different major genres of folk music. The purpose of these classifications is to help listeners browse music that suits their tastes.

Sometimes we songwriters approach topics that seem just too huge to deal with: Peace, Environment, Civil Rights, Economy, Prejudice. It is not easy, of course, to write a song with such a large perspective. To bring order to complex thoughts, we often look to "divide" or "classify" our topics as a way to break them down so that they can be analyzed.

For instance, say you are big into the environmental movement. This is a movement that is into conservation. It is scientific, it is social, it is political. The Environment is way too large to contemplate in one song. So you decide to focus on the social aspect. You want to encourage people to think about their actions and how they affect our world. You like the word "sustainable", but then find it is a big word in the scope of environmental issues. So you might break that down into categories: reduce fossil fuels, buy local, build "green", etc. Once you narrow your choice of topic into a manageable classification, you just might be able to get to writing that song because it is much more likely you can achieve your purpose of getting people to think sustainably.

Earlier I mentioned Bill Steele's song *Garbage*. This is a song that benefits from classification. The song focuses on the things we throw away, our waste, illustrating just one part of the environmental issue, but doing it well.

Another example of this technique is *Locally Grown* by John Forster and Tom Chapin. Like Steele's song, it focuses on just this one category of the environment: buying food locally. This mode of development allows for the use of specific detail. The lyrics dwell only on Produce and explain how far things travel to get to our stores. When they are done tracing the travels of the apple from Tasmania, and the berry from Chile, they admonish you to think twice about the pie that is enlarging our carbon footprint and to shop, grow, and eat locally.

By dividing environmental issues, and using this limited example, the writers are able to make a definite point with concrete references within the necessary time limit and attention span of the audience.

Classification and Division can be used to help take a stand on many complicated issues. Is there a difference between banning guns and gun control? Songwriters must face this question. Some people hear Cheryl Wheeler's *If It Were Up to Me* as simply that – take away all the guns. Ban them. However, if one looks more closely at the lyrics, she appears to be ruminating on the possible ways that children get hold of guns and says to heck with the excuses. (According to cherylwheeler.com, Cheryl said that is exactly where the idea for the song came from). Keep guns out of the hands of children. Now that is gun *control*. It might not be easy to ban of all our guns, but with the right laws we can certainly make adults do a better job at keeping them away from impressionable children. This makes her song much more effective than just calling for a "ban" on guns, because it allows for argumentative details that are more difficult to cover in a short time.

How we go about classifying and dividing depends, as usual, upon our audience and our purpose. The classification-division strategy is especially helpful as we pre-write. It can provide a great brainstorming tool. If you are overwhelmed by your topic, then sitting down and brainstorming by breaking down this larger topic into classifications can be enormously helpful.

I wrote a song about the harmful chemicals in fragrances and body products called *Sweet Poison*. There are many dangers to our environment that are caused by the things we often do unthinkingly. We are all aware of the importance of recycling, or reducing car emissions, or reducing packaging. All of these are hard to fit into a song. By taking one aspect of danger in our environment, I focused on the scents we find in our personal and household products on a daily basis. I use narrative structure as the format and the song combines narrative with illustrations, using product names that people will recognize.

The immediate impact on the allergic is stressed (achoo!) but beneath the surface is the message that many people are greatly affected by scent and it just might impact your love life!

See more about this song in Section XI, p. 162.

Process Analysis

"Process analysis is a form of technical writing and expository writing designed to convey to the reader how a change takes place through a series of stages."

~www.dictionary.com

By defining a process, showing how something works, we can aid our listeners in the "how to". This is called a directional narrative. Process can come in handy for some purposes; for instance, there is a children's song by Patty Shukla called *I'm Gonna Make a Cake* that details the method, ingredients, and the steps used in making a cake. It seems most likely that the video that accompanies the song is important, as is the use of the song for teaching numbers. What is Patty's purpose in detailing the process of cake making? I doubt that she intends it as a strict recipe she expects people to follow. For instance, one step adds a stick of butter – but the song doesn't mention it is melted at that point.

Later, she says to "use your hands" to pour it into the pan when the video shows the more desirable use of a spatula (held by hands!) for that purpose. She is also careful to make sure the children know that Mom is the one who should put the cake into the oven and take it out. (In writing a Process Analysis, it is *always* important to note any particular things that we are NOT supposed to do). So, is the song intended to be an exact recipe for cake baking or an approximate one for teaching children how to count? I would say the latter. In this it excels. On examining this song that most closely resembles a "how to" process song, it becomes apparent how difficult it is to explain a process like this in song.

However, most process in creative writing is not directional, but rather an extended chronological illustration. For example, listen to Joni Mitchell's *The Circle Game*. The extended illustration shows the process of a child growing into someone who begins life eager to get older, but eventually wants to "slow the circle down". The song is not a series of steps, but of process narrative. Like the numbers in *Make A Cake,* the nouns and tense show us the passing of time:

"Yesterday a child came"/ "Then the child moved ten times round the seasons"/"Sixteen springs, sixteen summers gone now"/"Years spin by and now the boy is twenty"

We don't know the age of the child when the song starts, but it is an age where the small things provoke wonder, tears, and fears. Later it is mentioned what happens when the child is ten, sixteen, and twenty. I used to sing this song often and it occurred to me that Joni switches from past to present tense when the child gets to sixteen, before the final age of twenty. Why not stay in the past tense until the end? Maybe it was just to rhyme "gone now" and "long now". But this doesn't bother the audience who is not that analytical, and since the chorus is always in the present (the seasons they go round and round) it doesn't jar the senses with the tense shift. When the song is over we know we have been taken through the process of growing up with its life lessons.

E.B. White and his wife Katharine are credited with saying , "Explaining a joke is like dissecting a frog. You understand it better but the frog dies in the process."

Human minds work differently. What is funny to one person is not funny to another, and analyzing why doesn't help. You are never going to be funny to everyone so it doesn't help to take a scalpel to a joke. People either get it or they don't. The purpose of some process analysis is to convey steps that can be emulated by the listener. However, when we attempt to comment, in a song, about some larger philosophical or sociological process, we don't really want people to analyze it - we want them to feel it. When we hear *Circle Game, or "Cat's In the Cradle"* by Harry Chapin, we don't think, "Oh, that's a process," we just understand the meaning because it has been presented in a way that makes sense.

In going over the hundreds of songs I have written, I can't find a single one that I can label a true process analysis. A process talks us through steps in a logical way as exemplified by the songs I talked about above. More likely, I find that I often use process as a part of what is know as "causal analysis"—
the examining of what causes another thing to happen, or what effect is the outcome of an event. As illustrated well in *Cat's in the Cradle,* Process and Cause and Effect are greatly related.

CAUSE AND EFFECT

"When two things occur successively we call them cause and effect if we believe one event made the other one happen. If we think one event is the response to the other, we call it a reaction. If we feel that the two incidents are not related, we call it a mere coincidence. If we think someone deserved what happened, we call it retribution or reward, depending on whether the event was negative or positive for the recipient. If we cannot find a reason for the two events' occurring simultaneously or in close proximity, we call it an accident. Therefore, how we explain coincidences depends on how we see the world. Is everything connected, so that events create resonances like ripples across a net? Or do things merely co-occur and we give meaning to these co-occurrences based on our belief system?

~ Liezi, Lieh-tzu, A Taoist Guide to Practical Living

"Shallow men believe in luck or in circumstance. Strong men believe in cause and effect."

~ Ralph Waldo Emerson

Causal analysis is one way we fulfill our human need to connect things. If we can make sense out of what causes what, and the effects those causes have, we feel more secure and focused. It is important in analyzing a subject that we don't "jump to conclusions." A famous logical fallacy is called "post hoc, ergo propter hoc" – therefore this, because of that. This fallacy occurs when we arrive at a conclusion based on correlation instead of true cause and effect. For instance: "Our cities have more immigrants from Mexico. The crime rate has increased. Therefore, Mexican immigrants are to blame." More information is needed before drawing this conclusion. This is an error of logic. However, showing cause and/or effect can be a very helpful mode when trying to make a point.

Example: The song, *Methamphetamine*, by Ketch Secor and David Rawlings indicates that poverty and corruption leads to drug addiction in the coal mining regions. The song is simple, and the correlation between selling meth and going hungry for some, and the resulting ravages of drug addiction in others is drawn quickly. Mama and Papa "ain't hungry anymore." That *anymore* relates to one cause and effect in this line: they were hungry (the cause) they aren't anymore (effect). Other causes of selling meth are the choice between the coalmine and the National Guard. In general, it is the lack of opportunity for those in the region that is a cause.

But meth has a different effect for others. The chorus highlights the impact on those who buy:

It's gonna rock you like a hurricane
It's gonna rock you till you lose sleep
It's gonna rock you till you're out of a job
It's gonna rock you till you're out on the street
It's gonna rock you till you're down on your knees
It's gonna have you begging pretty please
It's gonna rock you like a hurricane
Methamphetamine

Mac Davis' song, *In the Ghetto,* is also an example of a causal analysis song. In fact, the original title of the song was *The Vicious Circle.* The message is that the violence in the poor parts of the city is caused by poverty. In the beginning, a child's "hunger burns" and that is the way the song ends as well.

The Boy He Used to Be by Jane Fallon

This song, published on my CD, *Gemini Rising in a Patchwork Sky* is a cause and effect narrative that relates a history of PTSD.

We first see the soldier first as a happy well-adjusted young man who is sent off to war; he then experiences some very tough battles, and comes home a different person. In the second verse, his youth and innocence is mentioned again, this time giving insight into his sweet, non-combative character.

I then "flashback" to his even earlier youth relating an incident that truly shows his inherent character of pacifism; the lack of violence in his nature is another detail that would show why having to kill or be killed "tore him up inside."

The third verse gives insight into his postwar life. He seemed to have adjusted back into civilian life, was godly and a good family man. But the chorus has been telling us about the affect that the war had on him. He never would be that "boy he used to be". Finally, the lasting effect that his war experiences had upon him is mentioned: he "drank himself to death".

This song is my interpretation of what might have happened to a family member whom I never knew well because he died when I was young. I could only suppose. But I was gratified when a local war veteran who wrote often about his Viet Nam experiences assured me that this picture, one of the veteran who returned home and slowly self-destructed was accurate. He asked me, "Did he leave his family? Find another woman?" I said, "Yes". He said, "That is a very common thing. Men can't cope and the women they left can't cope, so they look for a new, more compassionate shoulder, that is either a woman or bottle, or both."

Lyrics, Section 11, p. 169.

COMPARISON

"Why do you sit there looking like an envelope without any address on it?"

~ Mark Twain

"Anxiety's like a rocking chair. It gives you something to do, but it doesn't get you very far."

~ Jodi Picoult, *Sing You Home*

"I'm a little pencil in the hand of a writing God, who is sending a love letter to the world."

~ Mother Teresa

"Life is a moderately good play with a badly written third act."

~ Truman Capote

Most of us know the general meaning of this mode. We find understanding in looking for the differences and similarities in events happening around us.

Comparison in songwriting can be as direct as looking at two objects or people using similar criteria. For instance, in Townes Van Zandt's song, *Pancho and Lefty*, we hear the story of two outlaws and how they started and ended their lives differently. Poet Edwin Arlington Robinson wrote of Richard Cory, comparing his outward demeanor ("he glittered when he walked") to his eventual surprising ending ("one night he went home and put a bullet to his head") which forms a comparison of the man on the outside and the man on the inside.

In *Yesterday*, Paul McCartney uses comparison in its most understandable sense, and each comparison is complete:

(then) all my troubles seemed so far away
(now) it looks as if they're here to stay
(then) life was such an easy game to play
(now) I need a place to hide away

I love the simple symmetry in *Yesterday.* It reads like an essay in its balance. However, it is more common to hear poetic forms of comparison in songwriting, especially when we are concerned with trying to convey abstract qualities like love, poverty, and injustice. We try to find ways for our audience to understand what these abstract words mean to us.

To do this, we use very special form of comparison that is used in songwriting and poetry is called "metaphor". Through metaphor, we make a comparison of two unlike things in order to aid in explanation. We saw an example of this earlier in Lewis Allan's *Strange Fruit.* Bob Dylan's "A Hard Rain's Gonna Fall" relies on imagery and uses 'hard rain' as a metaphor for coming injustice, war, and pollution in the world. Neil Young was a "miner for a heart of gold", and Elvis cried, "you ain't nothin' but a hound dog".

Guest Artist: Pat Wictor

Pat Wictor first burst on the folk and acoustic scene as an innovative slide guitarist known for fresh and memorable interpretations of traditional and contemporary songs. He has since made his mark as a singer-songwriter penning lean and poetic songs that incorporate - and subvert - rural blues and gospel traditions.

An American by birth, Pat's early years were spent in Venezuela, Holland, Norway, England, and East Texas. His time abroad gave him the perspective of a world citizen, and set him on a journey to understanding America - and his own American-ness - through music. Through these early experiences, he gained an appreciation for taking different paths to arrive at the same destination.

Recognition and honors have followed Pat for years: he won the Falcon Ridge Emerging Artist Showcase, was nominated for Emerging Artist of the Year by the Folk Alliance, was nominated for Gospel Song of the Year by the Independent Music Awards, and was a finalist in the Kerrville New Folk songwriting contest. His CD "Sunset Waltz" reached #2 on the Folk-DJ charts, and "Heaven is so High" and "Waiting for the Water" both reached #4.

For the past five years he's been touring nationally as one third of *Brother Sun*, the powerful harmonizing trio with Joe Jencks and Greg Greenway, garnering critical acclaim, a #1 CD on the Folk DJ charts, and a continent-spanning tour schedule.

You can find out more about Pat, and listen to his music at www.patwictor.com

Love is the Water by Pat Wictor © (Tell A Tale Music/BMI)

You say your heart's been turned to stone
You say you wanna be left alone
You say love only made you weep and moan
Well, let me tell you something that you know in your bones

Refrain:
Love is the water that wears down the rock
Love is the water that wears down the rock
Love is the power that won't be stopped
Love is the water that wears down the rock

You say your soul's like a dry riverbed
Stopped waiting for the water long ago, you said
You better pray all night for the rain instead
Love comes like a tidal wave, over your head

Refrain

You say, waiting for love takes too long
It dulls a sharp mind, weakens the strong
Well, you may be right, but you may be wrong
Cause love can make a mountain come tumbling down

Refrain

The river washes over every woman and man
Feet in the gravel, and mud in your hands
Nothing can stand against love's command
Every boulder turns into a grain of sand

In his song *Love is the Water,* songwriter Pat Wictor likens love to something we are familiar with: water. He carries the metaphor further by using water in a specific context. Over time, water erodes even the strongest of geologic formations. It is known to "wear down the rock." The rock is a symbol for a hardened heart.

Wictor creates a catchy and simple song that does what a good metaphor is supposed to do: be clear and be consistent. The comparisons between love and water create a vivid picture:

Love is the water that wears down the rock provides the general portrait, and that is repeated as the chorus. It is a river, he says, that washes over us all (Love is pervasive); nothing can stand against its command (Love is an unstoppable force like a raging rush of water). He does use one simile: Love comes like a tidal wave. He doesn't say "Love is a tidal wave". The reason for this is that the phrase completes the previous line: "You better pray all night for the rain instead [because] love comes like a tidal wave over your head." This is one thought, and the use of the simile is more effective here as it relates to the metaphor.

If we look at the use of the "rock" metaphor, Wictor is consistent there as well. He compares the heart to stone, the soul to the dry riverbed.

In the final analysis, when the water and rock come together, mountains come tumbling down and boulders become sand.

Wictor also makes great use of imagery. In the last verse he gives us a vivid, metaphorical picture of how love affects us all. There we are, standing in that river. Our feet may be in the gravel as we try to keep our hearts steadfast, but that resolve turns to mud by a force stronger than ourselves.

Guest Artist: Carl Cacho

Carl Cacho has firmly established himself as one of the most highly regarded performing songwriters in New England.

Boston Music Award Nominee for Outstanding new Singer Songwriter, winner of the Rose Garden Coffeehouse Singer/Songwriter Competition, finalist in the Kerrville Folk Festival, Telluride Troubadour and Boston Folk Festival songwriter contests, his songs and disarming performing style have made him a favorite at venues across the Northeast. Folk legend Tom Rush personally selected Carl to perform with him at a "Club 47" show at Harvard University's Sanders Theater and Carl was invited to participate in the Fifth Annual Martha's Vineyard Singer/Songwriter Retreat, started by Christine Lavin.

Written with stunning detail and clarity, Carl's songs draw the listener into focused snapshots of events and people that usually pass unnoticed. An eclectic mix of musical styles is evident throughout his work—bluegrass, blues, country and rock all make appearances, depending on the need of the lyric. His songs have been covered by many of his peers, including Jack Hardy, Kevin So, Stephanie Corby, Pat Wictor, Charlie Strater and Jimmy LaFave. His album “Spark” features duets with Jimmy LaFave and Kris Delmhorst as well as appearances by Ellis Paul and Mark Erelli. It was one of the top 10 played albums on Folk Radio for three consecutive months.

Visit Carl’s website at www.carlcacho.com

Bluest of Things, Carl Cacho ©2002, Black Holler Music

There's blue that's as sweet as my sister's eyes
There's blue that's as free as the wide-open sky
There's blue deep as the ocean where the tall ships fly
There's blue that's as lonesome as a coyote's cry
There's blue that's as pure as a church bell's ring
But the blue in my heart is the bluest of things

There's blue that's as dark as the moon going down
There's blue that's as hard as the steel rails through town
There's blue soft as the ashes of the old house burned down
There's blue that's as steady as the world spinning round
There's blue that's as bright as a new diamond ring
But the blue in my heart is the bluest of things

There's blue that's as long as the path that you choose
There's blue that's as gone as the true love you lose
There's blue sad as the mud on a gravedigger's shoes
There's blue that's as desperate as a man that's accused
There's blue that's as rough as the bad news you bring
But the blue in my heart is the bluest of things

Simile

"A simile, to be perfect, must both illustrate and ennoble the subject; must show it to the understanding in a clearer view, and display it to the fancy with greater dignity; but either of these qualities may be sufficient to recommend it."

~Samuel Johnson, Pope: Lives of the Poets.

Another form of comparison, similes (comparisons using 'like' or 'as') is often used as well. A simile likens two things that on the surface seem different."

In "Bluest of Things" the theme of the song is metaphorical. The word "blue" in its first, most obvious meaning is a color. In a second meaning is "depressed, or sad". Carl's emphasis is on this kind of blue, the sadness that is the theme of the song.

The intent of the song is to reinforce this abstraction, this feeling: there is nothing as blue as the way his heart is feeling at the moment. To achieve that, he chooses a series of concrete images in order to make the abstract easy to grasp.

What makes Carl's song unique is that it is all descriptive definition. There is no plot. There are no characters, no facts, no proposals or solutions. No chorus. No bridge. Though it is packed with adjectives, the adjectives are embedded in visual imagery. It would not be enough to say that blue is: sweet, free, deep, lonesome, and pure etc. The continuation of the comparison completes it.

It is important to note that while using simile, you do not create a simile by simply using the words 'like' or 'as'. Comparing things that are too like is a simple comparison. By its nature, the simile should compare unlike things. The literary biographer Samuel Johnson likened simile to two lines approaching each other from a great distance and then finally converging. On the other hand, two lines that run parallel, never far separated and never joined, would be a simple exemplification.

Carl uses a variety of techniques. His is a "thinking song". The appreciation of the lyrics increases each time we hear them.

At first, I paused when I heard "a blue that's as bright as a new diamond ring." I was uncertain about the comparison. How is a diamond blue and how does that blue equate to a sad feeling? It eventually made sense to me in this way:

A blue diamond is rare – it is unique. People have questioned the authenticity of blue diamonds. In this context, this "blue" that the writer is explaining is a unique feeling and a confusing one. Carl does what most good poets do – he leaves it up to the audience to make the abstract concrete, and by comparing the abstract to the concrete, he hopes to explain a feeling.

Definition

"What's in a name? That which we call a rose
By any other name would smell as sweet."

~Romeo and Juliet (II, ii, 1-2)

"The beginning of wisdom is the definition of terms."

~ Socrates (attributed)

It is sometimes important to define your terms, or to make sure that the term you are using is defined consistently. Are you concerned about "global warming" or "climate change"? Is there a difference? You might need to make that clear.

The term "racism" is defined as the belief that a culture or race is inferior, while "racial bias" relates to people's unconscious adherence to make decisions based on stereotype. Janice Ian's *Society's Child* contains an explicit message of racism, so the details chosen reflect that.

She called you 'boy' instead of your name/ honey,
He's not our kind/ teachers laugh/ smirking stares/
They say I can't see you anymore

The song paints a picture of pure racism. Whites see blacks as inferior and believe the races should not mix.

On the other hand, the story of *Hurricane* by Bob Dylan and Jacque Levy reflects the racial bias of a society that allows a black man to be convicted of a crime he didn't commit just because he is black. It takes time to relate the story, but the details always reflect that Rubin Carter was obviously framed through racial injustice:

All of Rubin's cards were marked in advance
The trial was a pig-circus, he never had a chance
The judge made Rubin's witnesses drunkards from the slums
To the white folks who watched he was a revolutionary bum
And to the black folks he was just a crazy nigger
No one doubted that he pulled the trigger
And though they could not produce the gun
The D.A. said he was the one who did the deed
And the all-white jury agreed.

Each song takes a different approach to get the purpose across, and uses words and phrases that best relate to its definition of race and its issues.

Walking Wounded by Jane Fallon

What does the phrase "walking wounded" mean? Well, I found out that it is currently Internet slang for "abused", primarily domestic abuse. I certainly wasn't thinking of that when I wrote this song ten years ago, with the events of 9/11 still in my head. I had been invited to write a song for an ADAA (Anxiety and Depression Association of America) support group, and the term seemed to fit.

However, technically, it began as a battlefield term. The "walking wounded" are those who have been injured but can still walk. That seems simple. But the walking wounded were also those with relatively low priority. It was more important to address those who needs were immediate – the dying.

Noting this, it seems appropriate that the domestic-abuse activists have commandeered the phrase. Women who have been abused often live emotionally wounded without attention. It is in that vein that I define the term in my song.

To illustrate the term, I use four different scenarios (Illustration). I start with the chorus in the hope that people will understand what is coming.

The first scenario is that of parents who are informed their son has died at war. They will be forever changed.

The second portrays a woman who observed the devastation as the Twin Towers were brought down in 9/11. What she saw impacted her greatly and she drowns the pain and her loss of faith in people with a bottle.

The third scene was somewhat personal, as I had just helped my mother die and then spent time with my dad who was dazed at her lost.

I try to tie it together with the chorus, about another type of walking wounded: the homeless. They go on everyday, simply existing, and often invisible to most. The homeless man also becomes a metaphor for the other three examples. Those who live with their emotional wounds daily find ways to go on, although it never truly gets rid of the pain, but it does allow them to hope.

I have had good reaction with the song, but I think it is one that requires much of the audience. First, they need to understand that there are three separate stories here. I use this technique frequently, and know that it can be confusing to the audience. In this case, by shifting person (a couple, a woman, a man) I hope to aid in understanding.

However, after I sang this once a man came up to me and said that "Tanqueray Gin" is very expensive and not likely to be in the hands of a hobo. He had not understood the distinctions at first hearing, and since the chorus is the most prevalent part of the song, had understandably focused on it.

I did not edit anything based on his comment, because I think that on a second hearing he would understand. While it is important to make things as easy on our listeners as possible, it is rare that any listener "gets" everything in the first hearing – in fact, likely it is impossible. And while songs should always be accessible at some point, it is not unusual for the process to take more than one listen. I discuss this at more length in the section on Editing.

You can read the lyrics and further analysis of this song in Section XI, p. 167.

Persuasion

Rhetoric may be defined as the faculty of observing in any given case the available means of persuasion. This is no a function of any other art.

~ Aristotle

Persuasion is often more effectual than force. ~ Aesop

Not Brute Force but Persuasion and Faith are kings of this world.
~ Thomas Carlyle

So now we arrive at what Aristotle felt rhetoric was all about: persuasion. Persuasion differs from argumentation in that, in order to argue, we use clear thinking and logic to convince our audience to accept our point of view. When we rely mostly on emotional and dramatic appeals, we are leaning more towards persuasion.

While often a combination of both is employed, for purpose-oriented writers, this mode is most likely to achieve their goals; it is the most all-encompassing, because in order to be persuasive, we most likely must use some of the other modes in order to provide evidence.

> *This Land is Your Land* (Woody Guthrie) uses a narrative structure combined with a lot of great description to make his point that America is for everyone.
>
> Pete Seeger uses narrative and process in his anti-war song, *Where Have All the Flowers Gone.*
>
> *Plane Wreck at Los Gatos* or *Deportee* by Woody Guthrie uses description, narration, definition, and illustration to create an argument against the way immigrants were being treated.

In addition, persuasion will incorporate one or more of the appeals of logos, pathos, and ethos, with pathos being the most common because of its immediate effect on the audience.

Perhaps there is no more contentious argument in American culture today than what it means to be an American, and no greater symbol than a large sculpture that sits in New York Harbor called The Statue of Liberty.

"The New Colossus" by Emma Lazarus

Not like the brazen giant of Greek fame,
with conquering limbs astride from land to land;
Here at our sea-washed, sunset gates shall stand
a mighty woman with a torch, whose flame
is the imprisoned lightning, and her name Mother of Exiles.
From her beacon-hand
glows worldwide welcome; her mild eyes command
the air-bridged harbor that twin cities frame.
"Keep, ancient lands, your storied pomp!" cries she
with silent lips. "Give me your tired, your poor,
your huddled masses yearning to breathe free,
the wretched refuse of your teeming shore.
Send these, the homeless, tempest-tost to me.
I lift my lamp beside the golden door!" [8]

Sculptor Frederic Bartholdi called his famous statue "Liberty Enlightening the World," but it very soon became know as The Statue of Liberty, and to many, Our Lady of the Harbor.The statue has become an undeniable cultural symbol of America. The statue has become a metaphor for the fight for freedom, but more importantly she stood at the gateway to millions of immigrants that arrive in America in the 1800's. The Jewish American Poet, Emma Lazarus, saw this sculpture as representing the dreams and aspirations of those who came to America seeking freedom and wrote a poem that will be forever associated with the statue. (www.nps.gov)

Our Lady in Music

I remember singing Irving Berlin's "Give Me your Tired, Your Poor" in middle school. Written in 1949 and called "Miss Liberty", it is the first instance I can find for a musical setting of the famous poem. Exactly when people began referring to it as "Our Lady of the Harbor" I don't know, but the most famous use of this line in contemporary music seems to have been in Leonard Cohen's 1966 song "Suzanne":

And the sun pours down like honey
On our lady of the harbour
And she shows you where to look
Among the garbage and the flowers

However Cohen's song is not about the New York Harbor, but rather the Old Port of Montreal. It refers to a statue of the Virgin Mary on the Notre Dame de Bon Secour Chapel. The song is not about freedom, and the line is just a poetic line of place.

Whether or not Cohen's song encouraged its use in later songs by many songwriters including folksingers like David Crosby and Si Kahn, classical composer Lee Hoiby or Country Singer, Waylon Jennings, I don't know. But it is so obvious why the phrase became common in our cultural lexicon. It is highly evocative.

Much has been written about the statue, and some argue it is not a symbol of freedom for African Americans or even for the women who were not allowed to go to the dedication, it is typically regarded as a beacon of hope for new immigrants.

"I saw the Statue of Liberty. And I said to myself, "Lady, you're such a beautiful! [sic] You opened your arms and you get all the foreigners here. Give me a chance to prove that I am worth it, to do something, to be someone in America." And always that statue was on my mind." [9]

Guest Writer: Joe Jencks

About Joe Jencks: Joe Jencks is an international touring performer, songwriter, entertainer, and educator, based in Chicago, IL. From venues like Carnegie Hall and Lincoln Center in New York, to coffee houses, festivals, spiritual communities, and schools, Joe has spent the last 12 years touring full time. His songs have traveled to every continent via his own performances, radio, CDs, web casts, and other musicians. He is noted for his unique merging of musical beauty, social consciousness, and spiritual exploration. Jencks weaves a diverse web of stories with brilliant musical skill, ensnaring even the most rigid of hearts, inviting them to open. His songs invite us to live inside of our passions and our beliefs.

In 2010, Jencks co-founded a dynamic new trio called *Brother Sun* with colleagues Greg Greenway and Pat Wictor. The trio performs widely throughout the United States and Canada, and their current recording "Some Part of the Truth" debuted at #1 on the Folk DJ Chart in March and remained there in April.

In addition to the recording debuting at #1, Jencks's song "Lady of the Harbor" (track 1 on the recording) also debuted at #1. Brother Sun's self titled debut recording also rose to the top of the Folk DJ chart spending 13 of 15 months on the chart and made the "Best of 2011" list for over a dozen radio stations in the US. Fusing, Folk, Roots, Blues, Pop, Jazz, Rock, and a cappella singing, Brother Sun is an explosion of musical diversity and harmony, in the finest of male singing traditions.

See www.joejencks.com and www.brothersunmusic.com for more information.

Lady Of The Harbor By Joe Jencks

From far away, and distant lands
The tempest tossed with hopeful hearts and calloused hands
Reach for the light, the torch held high
And cast their gaze upon the Lady of the Harbor

And she welcomes them with open arms
she says let my children in
Shine on, Shine on , Oh you Lady of the Harbor

And so it was, with my own kin
They sailed from Sweden and from France, and Ireland
Their earthly cares, packed in their bags
They cast their gaze upon the Lady of the Harbor

And she welcomes them with open arms
she says let my children in
Shine on, Shine on, Oh you Lady of the Harbor

Now we're locking down the borders and we're filling up the jails
And we say they don't belong
How conveniently do we forget
That we've all come to sing the same sweet song

Will the dream, survive the strain
Will huddled masses have a chance to learn it's sweet refrain
Or will we fall, into our fears
And turn our backs against the Lady of the Harbor.

And she welcomes them with open arms
she says let my children in
Shine on, Shine on , Oh you Lady of the Harbor

One of the most evocative songs that uses the phrase, Lady of the Harbor, comes from songwriter and performer, Joe Jencks. The use of **pathos**, **ethos**, and **logos** is highly evident in his song that warns against enacting strict laws that would deny future immigrants the right to enter our country.

Is the phrase passé, just because it has been used before? One cannot copyright a title, and the very fact that it is well known and ubiquitous increases its value as the focal point for Joe's message. Any American will know what Joe is referring to, and only the most die-hard folk fan would have any chance of mistaking it for a Leonard Cohen line.

The largest persuasive element is pathos. Joe draws upon the timeworn and verifiable of those images of our past:

Hopeful hearts and calloused hands/
Earthly cares packed in their bags/

He refers specifically to the Lazurus poem through the use of carefully selected phrases:

"Tempest Tossed", and "huddled masses"

The effect is to hit at that place right in the middle of our hearts **(pathos)** as we envision those hard-working, careworn, people of the earth, seeking asylum from tyranny and poverty.

The gist of the argument arrives in the third and fourth verses and also relies on **pathos**. In contrast, we are "locking down the borders" and "filling up the jails"; he refers to "the dream" and twice mentions the sweetness of the song of freedom.

When the song is sung, with its soaring melody, it is impossible to not be touched emotionally.

But Joe doesn't rest there. Through the use of **ethos**, he gives credibility to his point. He mentions that he is the descendent of immigrants from Sweden, France, and Ireland. His lineage gives him some right to speak about the people he advocates for. He also creates what we call "homophily". This simply means that we tend to bond with others like ourselves.

It is commonly accepted that, except for the American Indian, all Americans are immigrants from other places. Joe says in essence, "We are all the same, and I am one of you." In fact, the use of the pronoun "we" instead of using the passive voice, or saying "you" also creates that **"more ethos"** bond. He is not blaming or attacking. This isn't about individuals, it is about America and we are all in it together.

Lastly, Joe uses just a hint of **logos**. He relies on Artistotle's famous "enthymeme". Previously I defined an enthymeme as a logical structure where one part of the syllogism is left unstated.

> **Major Premise**: The Statue of Liberty is symbolic of the freedom and liberty that America is all about
>
> **Minor Premise**: People seeking freedom and liberty are welcomed in America
>
> **Conclusion**: It goes against what our country is all about if we deny access to those seeking freedom and liberty.

The major premise is left unstated in Joe's song. He assumes, rightfully, that the audience will recognize this symbol and what she stands for. His syllogism makes the point that if we agree with the major premise and we agree with the minor premise, we must accept the conclusion. His reliance on the general acceptance of the statue's symbolism works within this logical context.

Now, the biggest argument that people might give against Joe's reasoning (remember the "other side") is that immigrants haven't always been welcomed. They haven't come in freely since the inception of Ellis Island, where they were often interred, inspected, and had their names changed. When they arrived, they were prejudiced against and sometimes indentured.

Well, Joe doesn't even try to answer these questions. Through the mode of Classification he narrows his topic. Verse three notes exactly what he is talking about. He isn't advocating totally free immigration. That is not his purpose. He is specifically addressing the current political train of thought that endorses totally shutting down our borders and putting illegal immigrants in jail without even a chance to become citizens.

At this point, he chooses the word (remember the importance of words) "conveniently". He could have said, "sadly" or "quickly" but "conveniently" provides just a little edge – there is a very soft admonition here. It is just a slap on the wrist, but it gives his argument strength. It is easy, he says, now that "we have ours" to refuse others entrance, to worry so much about ourselves, or economy, even our security (our fears) that we deny them the right to sail into the harbor guided by the mother of liberty.

Overall, Joe Jencks' *Our Lady of The Harbor* goes beyond the simple appeal to emotion and provides a strong case for immigration in less than five minutes

PART VI:

PUTTING IT TOGETHER

Using the Modes of Development
and the Rhetorical Triangle

There are many ways that people begin their songwriting process, but most will begin on one of the following ways:

1. Perhaps you only have **impetus**. In other words you have motivation and incentive. There is something moving you. You just want to write. If you have impetus but you don't really have a "reason" yet. In this case, just move straight to the modes of development. You can choose to tell a story, compare two things, define a term, etc. This is a great way to "brainstorm". Through this method you will find your "topic" and build from there.

2. Perhaps you have a **reason**. You have a cause, an event, or an action that propels you. For instance, you might want to write a song for your town's earth day. Or, maybe, you are going to participate in a songwriter's round where you must write on a specific theme. Maybe you would like to enter a songwriting contest. In this case, you most likely have both reason and a topic.

You can use your modes of development in order to find a direction for this topic.

You could research a story about it; you could define the term; you could compare your topic to something others might readily understand; you could narrow it down into a subtopic that is easy to handle. Perhaps your song might explain it, or illustrations give examples of it.

3. Maybe you want to start with a **purpose**. You have an aim, a plan, and an objective. Usually this option also means that you have a topic. Your big challenge is how to approach your audience. You analyze your audience and decide which of the appeals might best reach them. At the same time, you can examine the modes of development and experiment with a way to present your point. Will you tell a story that touches your audience's feelings? (**Pathos**) Will you use examples and facts to support a main idea and appeal to the audience's reason?

(**Logos**) Perhaps you will need to define your terms so that you audience will believe in your character. (**Ethos**)

4. One aspect of rhetorical process is that it always includes a **topic** and **audience**. It is obviously necessary to have something to communicate about and an audience to communicate with. And where do "you" – the speaker – fit? You are of course a necessary component of all of this, smack dab in the middle. However, this part of the triangle also comes with choices. Most audiences assume that because you are singing the song, it is based on personal experience. However, based on the purpose, you might find that another voice is more appropriate.

5. And finally, the **songwriting conventions** you choose (structure, melody, chords) will be added to this mix.

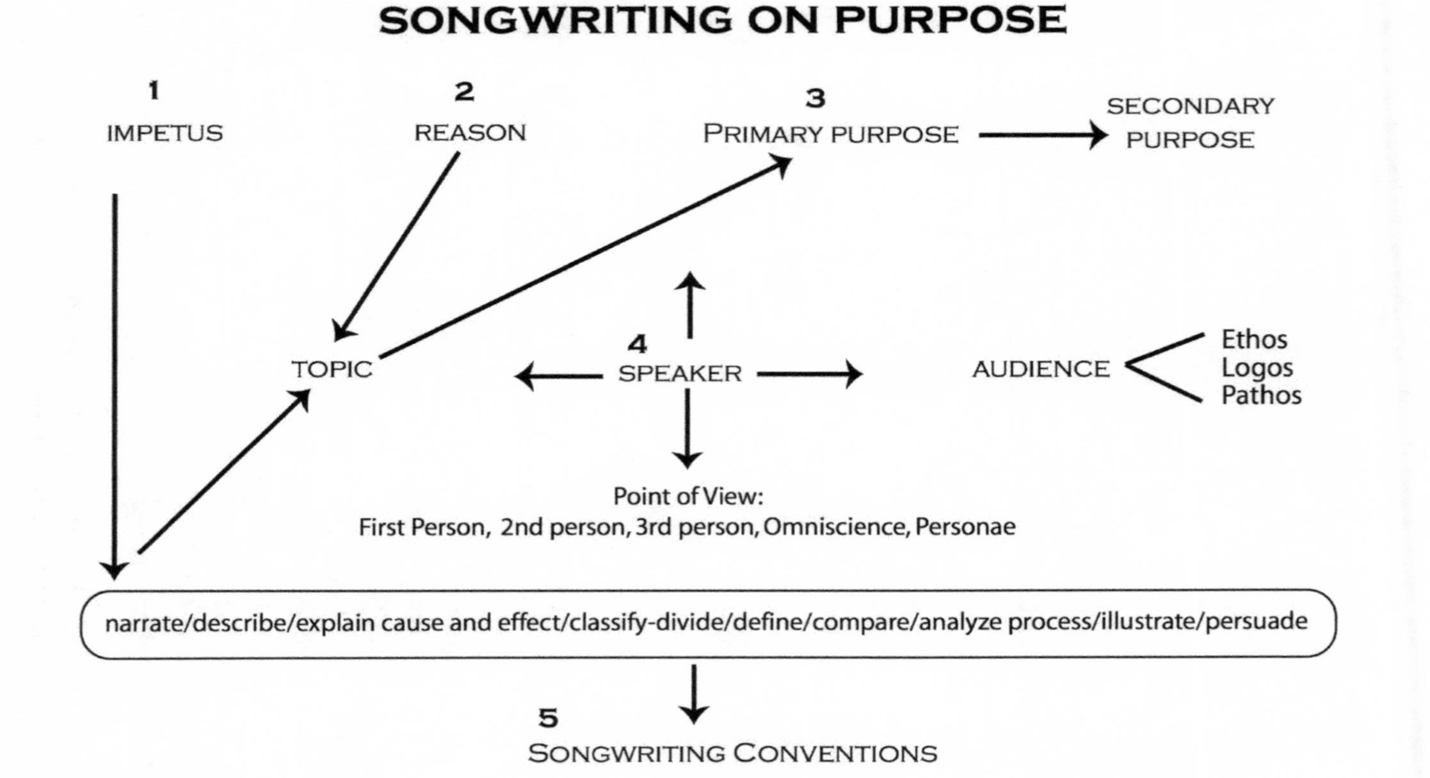
SONGWRITING ON PURPOSE
1
IMPETUS
2
REASON
3
PRIMARY PURPOSE
SECONDARY PURPOSE
TOPIC
4
SPEAKER
AUDIENCE
Ethos
Logos
Pathos
Point of View:
First Person, 2nd person, 3rd person, Omniscience, Personae
narrate/describe/explain cause and effect/classify-divide/define/compare/analyze process/illustrate/persuade
5
SONGWRITING CONVENTIONS

Mode of Development Worksheet	
Song Name	
Topic	
Speaker: Person/ Point of View	
Purpose: Inform/ Persuade/ Entertain	
Mode: Narration Description Cause/Effect Definition Process Illustration Persuasion Comparison Classification	
Appeals: Ethos Logos Pathos More Ethos	

VII: RESEARCH

"Doing research on the Web is like using a library assembled piecemeal by pack rats and vandalized nightly."

~ Roger Ebert

Getting information off the Internet is like taking a drink from a fire hydrant.

~ Mitch Kapor, variation of a quote by Jerome Weisner (Getting an education from MIT is like taking a drink from a fire hose.)

And of course, we have seen that picture of Abraham Lincoln next to the words, *"You can't believe everything you read on the Internet."*

These are great quotes, but as entertaining as it is to make fun of, and disparage, research in the Internet age, I prefer this quote:

> *The Internet is a big boon to academic research. Gone are the days spent in dusty library stacks digging for journal articles. Many articles are available free to the public in open-access journal or as preprints on the authors' website.*
> ~Nick Bostrom, Professor, Oxford University

In your quest to write purposefully, you will have a need for details. I discussed this earlier when I talked about whether or not your examples should definitely be factual. Research, and make sure your details are correct as possible. Using specific details and references in songs give them credibility, contributing to your **ethos** and also help to break writer's block. When stumped about adding content, research can be helpful.

As a graduate student in the 70's, I spent hours at the library. I would take my note cards and hole up on the 3rd floor of the University Library and not come out until it closed. Then I would use my notecards to type (yes, on a typewriter - not even an electric one) my papers. I would make sure to put a sheet underneath that told me where to stop if I had one, two or three footnotes. Although I was a pretty good typist, I still used my share of Wite-Out ® to correct mistakes and, if I was desperate, I used erasable "onion skin" paper. Are some of you following me out there?

Well, it is soooooo much easier today. Had I lived in the day of the Internet and computer terminals, who knows how many thoughtful academic theses I could have churned out. Maybe I would have even moved on to that PhD. I could have maintained my vitamin D3 levels as well by getting more of that Phoenix sunshine.

However, in this age of too much information, where anyone's an author, it is important to exercise special diligence when obtaining information from the World Wide Web. The librarians at the California State University in Chico, California came up with a standard that has since become highly popular and has been adopted by universities and colleges, and most likely some high schools, worldwide. It is called the "CRAAP Test."

THE CRAAP TEST

Does Your Web Site Pass the **CRAAP** Test?

Currency: The timeliness of the information.
When was the information published or posted?
Has the information been revised or updated?
Is the information current or out-of date for your topic?
Are the links functional?

Relevance: The importance of the information for your needs.
Does the information relate to your topic or answer your question?
Who is the intended audience?
Is the information at an appropriate level (i.e. not too elementary or advanced for your needs)?
Have you looked at a variety of sources before determining this is one you will use?

Authority: The Source of the Information
Who is the author/publisher/source/sponsor?
Are the author's credentials or organizational affiliations given? If yes, what are they?
What are the author's qualifications to write on the topic?
Is there contact information, such as a publisher or e-mail address?
Does the URL reveal anything about the author or source?
examples: .com .edu .gov .org Accuracy: The reliability, truthfulness, and correctness of the informational content.

Accuracy: Where does the information come from?
Is the information supported by evidence?
Has the information been reviewed or refereed?
Can you verify any of the information in another source or from personal knowledge?
Does the language or tone seem biased and free of emotion?

Are there obvious errors (spelling, grammar, etc.)?
Purpose: What is the purpose of the information?
To inform? teach? sell? entertain? persuade?
Do the authors/sponsors make their intentions or purpose clear?
Is the information fact? opinion? propaganda?
Does the point of view appear objective and impartial?
Are there political, ideological, cultural, religious, institutional, or personal biases?

There are good video tutorials on YouTube* such as this one by Johnson and Wales University at:

https://www.youtube.com/watch?v=lAWhE0mj69I

There are even songs that have been written about the test:

https://www.youtube.com/watch?v=HJ8ajc5FrT8

Created and produced by the University of Waikato Law Library, New Zealand. Love it. Wish I had written it.

https://www.youtube.com/watch?v=CMaLgec2XWY

Written and performed by Dr. Chad Bauman, at the time of this publication, a professor at Butler University in Indianapolis, IN.

*I apologize if any of these videos should at some time disappear. It happens! If that happens, go to the sources I underlined and see if you can find information there.

For a little more on where to find good lyrics, see References.

PART VIII: PERFORMANCE ASPECTS

Delivery, delivery, delivery.

Demosthenes' response when asked to name
the three most important components of rhetoric

Although this book is not meant to go into the intricacies of performance, its importance can't go totally unmentioned.

Of course, performance is important. Songs are a performance art and the delivery of the "purpose" by the "speaker" is tantamount to getting that purpose across. You can imagine, that given the scarcity of the written word for the average man in the time of the Greeks, and the total absence of recorded video and audio, that the delivery of the message was critical to it reception.

What I wouldn't give to travel back in time to hear blind Homer deliver his massive "Iliad" and "Odyssey" to a captive crowd. Were audiences more patient then? Most likely they were, simply because they had to be.

Our audiences, unfortunately, lack that patience. In order to keep their attention, to get your message across, you must pay attention to performance. Does this mean that you have be the world's best singer or instrumentalist? Not at all. However, if your performance distracts the listener from hearing the message, then some of your hard work will be in vain.

Consider the following once you have finely crafted your message:

- If your singing is distracting in any way, for instance if you have considerable trouble with pitch or enunciation, or if your particular style or gender doesn't convey what you want your audience to hear, consider finding a singer whose voice you feel matches the mood of your song and have him or her sing it. The same can be applied to your playing skills. We are conditioned to believe that we all need to be "triple threats" and somehow if we can't write, sing, and play everything ourselves excellently, we are somehow deficient. The famous composer, Irving Berlin, couldn't read or write music, and he had two transposing pianos so that he could play in just one key. You don't have to do it all.

- If your performing skills are very strong, find someone less skilled to sing your song to you. Listen objectively to find what song weaknesses your ability to perform has hidden. An exceptionally good performance can sometimes get in the way of your best effort.

- Pay attention to clarity. In a message song, the words should be easy to hear. Practice your diction.

- Definitely examine your songwriting devices such as rhyme and structure. Repetitions, such as those you find in choruses, help the audience pay attention.

- Practice your song, giving thought to nuance and body language. Think about taking a performance course from someone whose performances you admire.

- Play the song out the first time to a forgiving audience of friends and family, or to an objective audience such as a songwriting coach - in both cases you will feel less threatened.

Folk music is more forgiving than some song mediums because its roots are in the everyday man and woman who sang on their porches. However, today's Folk is a new medium, one of video, social media, the Internet and CD sales. Performance is often the first thing heard, and if it doesn't grab your audience, your words might not get a chance.

PART IX: COURTING THE MUSE

"The ideas come to me; I don't produce them at will. They come to me in the course of a sort of controlled daydream, a directed reverie. . . limitations provide a considerable spur to the imagination."

~Joseph Heller

Small rooms discipline the mind; large rooms distract it."

~Leonardo da Vinci

"It's good to have limits." Duke Ellington

"When forced to work within a strict framework the imagination is taxed to its utmost - and will produce its richest ideas. Given total freedom the work is likely to sprawl."

T.S. Eliot

What is the muse? I have often heard songwriters who have been on a dry spell creatively say something to the effect, "Oh thank you muse," or "I got a welcome visit from my muse", when they are able to finally write a song. These dictionary definitions remind us that inspiration is not creativity, however.

> Inspiration:
> *The process of being mentally stimulated to do or feel something, especially to do something creative.*
>
> Creativity:
> *The ability to transcend traditional ideas, rules, patterns, relationships, or the like, and to create meaningful new ideas, forms, methods, interpretations, etc.*

Inspiration is often identified with the word 'muse'. What is this muse thing? The nine muses in Greek mythology are deities that provide artists with the necessary inspiration for their creative acts. It is important to note that the muses give "inspiration" but not act of creation itself. Briefly, let me introduce you to the muses, Mother and daughters:

MNEMOSYNE: The Mother of the Muses and
the Goddess of Memory
CALLIOPE: Eloquence and Epic Poetry
CLIO: History and Writing
ERATA: Love Poetry
EURTERPE: Music
MELPOMENE: Tragedy
POLYHYMNIA: Oratory, sacred hymns, poetry
TERPSICHORE: Dance
THALIA: Comedy
URANIA: Astronomy and Science

It is evident that the ancient Greeks highly valued art and its inspiration and they made sense of that through creating Gods who made it all happen,. They saw poetry as coming out of that inspiration; in fact, they would not have seen poetry as being anything other than the act of making something new out of what was perceived to be nothing. The act of "creating" was a more foreign concept; they felt that visual artists operated from outside stimulus in accordance with the rules, and they liked it that way. They saw tangible art as a reflection of nature and of its discovery and not its invention.

However, as society progressed there were others who took a different view. Charles Batteaux (1713-1780) a French academician wrote, "*The human mind cannot create, strictly speaking; all its products bear the stigmata of their model; even monsters invented by an imagination unhampered by laws can only be composed of parts taken from nature.*"

And so it went back and forth at times throughout history. That the mind possesses imagination we seem to understand, but where it comes into play in the act of creation has provoked discussion throughout the ages.

This book deals a lot with form of thought and how we shape that using established models. Someone at a workshop asked me, "Well, what about inspiration? What if you are just inspired?" The ultimate conclusion among most modern philosophers is that feeling needs form and that there is no way in which we as human beings can separate our subconscious nature from our creative acts.

I have heard songwriters say that they write from dreams, and that these dreams are a form of unconscious, uncontrolled thought. But well-known psychologist, Rollo May (1909-1994) said that in analyzing dreams, he was "convinced that there is one quality that is always present, a quality I call a passion for form." He felt that

> *in creative endeavors the imagination operates in juxtaposition with form. When these endeavors are successful, it is because imagination infuses form with is own*

vitality. The question is: How far can we let our imagination loose? Can we give it rein? Dare to think the unthinkable? Dare to conceive of, and move among, new visions?

The Courage to Create, p. 128

The dilemma, then, that faces songwriters and poets particularly, is to decide where inspiration and form connect. Rollo's feeling is that they are never totally separate. We are all creatures of our past experiences and cannot separate ourselves from them. That brief moment of ecstasy that we call the muse breaks through our consciousness and for a moment we experience a sense of joy as creator. But this quickly moves to the need to shape that inspiration. "Order comes out of disorder, form out of chaos as it did in the creation of the universe." The paradox is that at that moment we also experience more vividly our own limitations."(Rollo, p. 123). Our sense of joy actually comes not from the inspiration but rather when we find that "particular form required" by our creation.

It is ironic. The Ancients created Gods and Goddesses to explain inspiration and in doing so actually contradicted their premise that poetry is not creation. Greek mythology sought to give shape to the shadows and the wind, to the changing of the seasons, to all that was unknown. But except in the annals of science fiction, the mind does not exist in a vacuum. Take joy in your inspiration; enjoy it; give it rein; think the unthinkable. But if you want others to understand that inspiration you must make order out of the chaos.

When you write a poem, you discover that the very necessity of fitting your meaning into such and such a form requires you to search in your imagination for new meanings. You reject certain ways of saying it; you select others, always trying to form the poem again. In your forming, you arrive at new and more profound meanings that you ever dreamed of.

Rollo May, The Courage to Create, p. 119

PART X: THE WRITING PROCESS

Inspiration, Form, and The Inner Critic

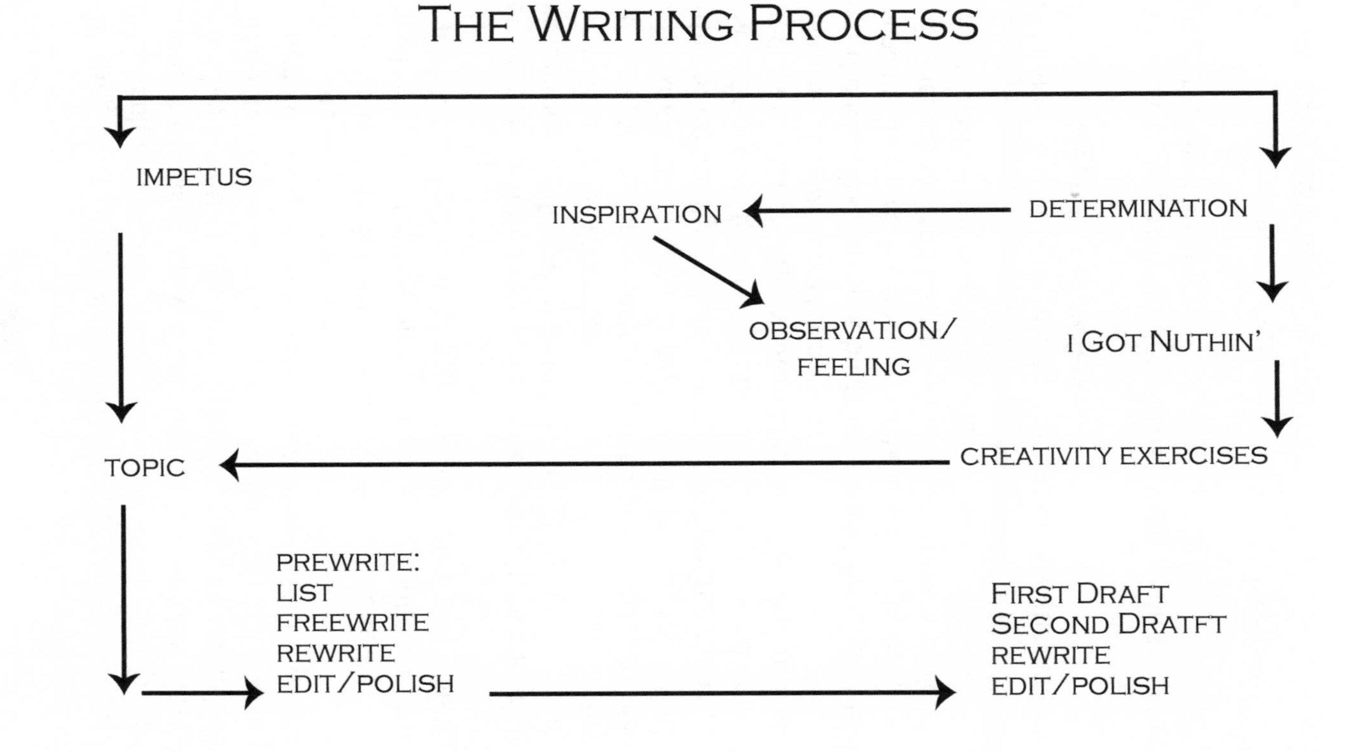
The Writing Process
Impetus
Inspiration
Determination
Observation/
Feeling
I Got Nuthin'
Topic
Creativity Exercises
Prewrite:
List
Freewrite
Rewrite
Edit/Polish
First Draft
Second Dratft
Rewrite
Edit/Polish

All writing is a process. Sometimes the process occurs mentally in such a way that we don't even know it is happening. Creative processes vary from person to person. Some songwriters begin with a chord progression and a rhythm. This in turn influences the words. Others begin with by writing words, either in a book or on a computer. Others let the words and music come at the same time.

You begin with an impetus (gotta write that song for the niece's wedding), an inspiration (I always get so lonely in the Fall), or just sheer determination (I am going to write a song, dammit!)

Impetus puts us one step ahead. We have a topic. At that point, we begin to decide what details we need by free writing, listing, or researching. When we are inspired, we have a very general topic that we refine through creativity exercises or free writing. If we are looking for a topic, perhaps we begin with free writing or creativity exercises, or find an impetus such as a prompt session. As we gain confidence in our topic we then list details and search for an organizational mode that best reflects and focuses the goal we have for our song.

When the song has taken a basic shape and form, and the ideas are basically there, we need to write and rewrite until the words and melody are the best they can be. Inspiration, Form, and the inner critic – this is how it goes:

1) We admit that our "inspiration" is not totally unaffected by the sum of our own experience.

2) We acknowledge that taking an idea from inspiration to creation requires form.

3) We understand that the form we choose will be dependent upon the goal we wish to accomplish.

4) We do what we can to collect the details, reasons, and examples to achieve that goal.

5) We write the first draft.

6) We use our personal ears, and trusted peer ears, for that draft.

7) We re-write or "tweak".

8) We take it to the masses via open mikes or trusted house concerts for reaction.

9) We re-write or "tweak".

10) We consider seeking critique from professional, "objective ears".

11) We rewrite or "tweak" until we think we have done our best.

At no time during this process do we let our "inner critic" tell us the song isn't working. However, we must allow that everything we write is not going to be our "best work". Some songs will just stand out and the rest become part of that vast body of work that we need to write but that might not stand the test of time.

If the lack of audience response to a song discourages you early because it is not "perfect" right away, and you let it go, you are doing your song a disservice.

If you think that inspiration is enough and form doesn't matter, then you are doing your inspiration a disservice. Remember your audience. They can't read between the lines. They can go back, via audio or video, to hear the song again, but if you have a true goal or purpose for your inspiration, then form is the one way to make that come across.

This "form" does not have to emulate any particular structure (i.e. verse, chorus, verse, bridge, chorus) or any traditional rhyme scheme. However, the purpose of your song is best served when you consciously select a form and presentation that is best suited to it.

If one form doesn't seem to work, then switch. Perhaps you have a narrative, but need to add more description. Maybe your narrative would be better told as a cause and effect. If your songs get long and complicated, maybe a look at division and classification would be a good thing. Are you clear on your definition of terms? Are you really writing about what you think you are writing about?

Is it possible to overthink? Can we sometimes edit too much? Of course we can. Often our process leads us back to a previous edit. (I highly recommend keeping all drafts). But to end the process too soon is to shortchange your song. Lyrics, music, and prosody – all are essential to songwriting and should be edited to best serve what purpose it is you are trying to achieve.

PART XI: RESOURCES

Song References:

It would be difficult to write a book about songwriting without examples. In order to provide examples I have chosen to use lyrics in their entirety only when given permission by the songwriter. However, I have referenced, and used a limited portion of lyrical texts without officially requesting permission. In some cases I requested permission but never heard back.

Used in the context of this book, the reference to lyrics is allowed under the doctrine of fair use: "the copying of copyrighted material for a limited and "transformative" purpose such as to comment upon, criticize, or parody a copyrighted work." (Rich Stim, Stanford University)

Since my intention in this document is not to compile a songbook of lyrics, but rather to use representative samples through which to explain processes involved in songwriting, I have chosen to include all of the lyrics to the songs I mention, especially if they are 1) well-known songs 2) mentioned only in passing and 3) available easily elsewhere.

Lyrics are ubiquitous on the Internet, in fact, they are among the most commonly searched-for terms; however, be aware that lyrics are often used without permission and violate copyright rules and contain inaccuracies.

Where to Find Lyrics

First, do your research and find the correct songwriter. When you "search" for lyrics, the first sites that will might include lyrics.com, azlyrics, metrolyrics etc. Most of these sites attempt to profit from the use of the lyric through advertising. I try to avoid these sites.

Look for sites that don't advertise except for the song itself (in other words, you can buy the song but not "xyz" product), and where all of the copyright information is included (songwriter and publisher). Some of these sites have a subscription fee, like Google Play. All of the lyrics for the songs I mention can be found somewhere in the digital universe.

Be wary of what sites you use for research, however. Many sites just copy inaccuracies from each other, the most common of which is confusing the author with the singer. If you are using the Internet for this information, research in more than one place. Eventually, you might see inconsistencies that cause you to double check the information.

One glaring discrepancy I found occurs in the lyrics for *America* by Neil Diamond. Trini Lopez' version (written by Diamond) was attributed to Sammy Johns who wrote a completely different song with the same title. The song was also attributed to the band Nice. If you look up Dylan's *Hurricane* on Google, you will be told it can be attributed to the writers and publishers of rap artist Mos Def's song of the same name.

The best place to obtain permission to use lyrics is from the songwriter or his/her publisher. Usually you can find this information on the songwriter's website. This would be the best way to find lyrics from a writer who is not signed to a major publisher and where they are owned by the songwriter. If you can't find the lyrics printed, you might be able to find a YouTube video by the performing artist. These sometimes have ads, but at least you can see the original writer performing and get the best idea of what the lyrics are.

In the case of this book, I am assuming that the reader simply wishes to find lyrics in order to understand the processes the book is explaining. If you desire to use lyrics for another purpose, I suggest you look more deeply into fair use and copyright laws elsewhere.

There are many apps available for finding lyrics, such as MusicMatch. They don't have ads, but they are community based, and songs are submitted under the assumption of copyright compliance.

There is a reason we say "Google It". The Google search engine is, at this time, the best place to find lyrics and has partnered with the word's largest lyric licensing service Lyric Find (www.lyricfind.com) a company that will provide royalties to publishing companies and songwriters. According to their website they have amassed licensing from over 4,000 music publishers and in over 100 countries. However, even here there can be ambiguities, especially for older songs where the copyright may refer to a specific version of the song.

There are many hardcopy, published lyric collections, of both well known and lesser-known popular and traditional songs, that can be found for purchase at many booksellers, however the largest selection can still be found online. For performance rights of complete songs, the Harry Fox Agency is the place to go to receive permission to record them.

I have done my best to list the songs I have referred to in this book and give you a place to find the lyrics. Those without (*) cannot be found using the Google Search Engine.

As a last resort, for better-known songs, you can visit one of the many lyric sites available, with caveats.

SONGS USED AS EXAMPLES FOR MODES OF DEVELOPMENT:

LOGIC:

ENTHYMEME:

On The Eve of Destruction, P.F. Sloan/Steve Barri
© 1964, Universal Music Publishing Group

Short People, Randy Newman
© 1977 Sony/ATV Music Publishing LLC, Warner/Chappell Music, Inc, Universal Music Publishing Group, Downtown Music Publishing

DEDUCTION:

Something in the Rain, Tish Hinojosa
© 1992 Warner/Chappell Music, Inc

INDUCTION:

We Didn't Light The Fire, Billy Joel
© 1989 Universal Music Publishing Group

ETHOS:

Folsom Prison Blues, Johnny Cash
© BM Rights Management US, LLC, Warner/Chappell Music

Angel From Montgomery, (1971) John Prine
© Warner/Chappell Music Inc.

In The Ghetto, Mac Davis
© (1969) Imagem Music Inc.

PATHOS:

And the Band played Waltzing Matilda, Eric Bogle
© Peermusic Publishing

Who's Next, Tom Lehrer, © 1967, Tom Lehrer
https://www.youtube.com/watch?v=oRLON3ddZIw

* *Airline of our Times,* Jon Swenson, © 2011

Eighteen Holes, John Denver
© 2002, Hal Leonard Corporation
1992 Bootleg video here:
https://www.youtube.com/watch?v=3fbTGhDDL2g

Four Years of College, Ben Grosscup
https://www.youtube.com/watch?v=_sWosZ2qshc

PREACHING TO THE CHOIR:

Come to the USA, Ray Stevens, © 2010 Clyde Records, Inc.

America, Neil Diamond
© Sony/ATV Music Publishing, LLC. Universal Music Publishing Group

More Ethos:

**Garbage*, Bill Steele
(1972) A true folk song, Bill's original version has been added to over the years by Mike Agranoff and Pete Seeger among others.

Something in the Rain, Tish Hinojosa
© 1992, Warner Chappell Music, Inc.

Change Myself, Todd Rundgren, © 1991, Warner/Chappell Music, Inc.

Man in the Mirror, S. Garrett/G. Ballard
© 1988 Sony/ATV Music Publishing, LLC, Warner/Chappell Music Inc. Universal Publishing Group

Peace Train, Cat Stevens (Yusaf Islam)
© 1971 EMI Music Publishing, Sony/ATV Music Publishing LLC, Warner/Chappell Music, Inc, BMG Rights Management US, LLC

Lost Woman, Ani DiFranco
© 1990, BMG Rights Management US, LLC

Narrative:

Plot with a Twist:

**The Night The Lights Went out in Georgia*, Bobby Russell
© 1972 Bobby Russell, Published by Pixrus Music

**Cold Blood*, Mark Stepakoff, © 2013, Mark Stepakoff

Tone:

**America*, Paul Simon, © 1998 Paul Simon
© 2016 Sony Music Entertainment

Voice:

Third Person Omniscient:

Eleanor Rigby, Lennon-McCartney
© 1966 Sony/ATV Music Publishing LLC

Third Person Specific:

She's Got a Way With Words, Andrew P. Albert/ Marc Besson/Wyatt Earp
© 2106 Warner Music Nashville

Passive voice:

We Weren't Born to Follow, Jon Bon Jovi/Richie Sambora
© 2009 Sony/ATV Music Publishing LLC, Universal Publishing

FIRST PERSON:

Ode to Billie Joe, Bobby Gentry
©1967 Universal Music Publishing Group, Spirit Music Group

Desperados Waiting For a Train, Guy Clark.
© 1973 Warner/Chappell Music, Inc.

PERSONAE:

Cold Blood, Mark Stepakoff, © 2013, Mark Stepakoff

STRUCTURE:

FLASHBACK:

Honey, Bobby Russell, © 1968 Russell-Cason Music

REVERSE CHRONOLOGY:

Long Black Veil, Wilkin and Hill,
© 1959 Universal Music Publishing Group

DESCRIPTION:

SENSES:

Sunday Morning Coming Down, Kris Kristofferson
© 1969 Sony/ATV Music Publishing LLC

Jean, Rod McKuen. Robin Spielberg
© 1969 Warner/Chappell Music

The Way We Were, Hamlisch, Bergman and Bergman
© 1973 Sony/ATV Music Publishing LLC

Too Many Memories, Stephen Bruton
© 1997 BMG Rights Management US, LLC

Annie's Song, John Denver
© 1974 Alfred, Warner Chappell Music Inc,
Warner/Chappell Music, Inc.

SPECIFIC DETAIL:

Lonesome Whistle, Hank Williams and Jimmy Davis (1950)
© Peermusic Publishing, Sony/ATV Music Publishing LLC,
Warner/Chappell Music, Inc.

Try and Little Tenderness, Jimmy Campbell/Reg
Connelly/Harry Woods (1932)
© Peermusic Publishing, Sony/ATV Music Publishing LLC

Blue Eyes Cryin' the Rain, Fred Rose
© Peermusic Publishing, Sony/ATV Music Publishing LLC

DOMINANT IMPRESSION:

Strange Fruit, Abel Meeropol (Lewis Allen), Dwayne P.
Wiggins, Maurice Pearl,
© Warner/Chappell Music, Inc., Universal Music Publishing

DETAIL FOR A PURPOSE

Garbage, Bill Steele

ILLUSTRATION:

Grown Men Don't Cry, Douglas and Seskin
© Kobalt Music Publishing Ltd., Sony/ATV Music Publishing LLC

Imagine, John Lennon
© Sony/ATV Music Publishing LLC,
Universal Music Publishing Group, Downtown Music Pub.

Black Man, Stevie Wonder, Gary Byrd
© EMI Music Publishing, Sony/ATV Music Publishing LLC,
Universal Music Publishing Group

Living While Black, Mike Glick, © 2014 Mike Glick

Here's To the Mississippi, Phil Ochs (1965)
© Universal Music Publishing Group

Blowin' in the Wind, Bob Dylan, © Bob Dylan Music

DIVISION/CLASSIFICATION:

Locally Grown, Tom Chapin/John Forster

Garbage, Bill Steele

If It Were Up to Me, Cheryl Wheeler (1997)
http://www.cherylwheeler.com/songs/iiwutm.html
© Penrod And Higgins Music / Amachrist Music, ACF Music Group

DEFINITION:

* *Society's Child*, Janice Ian
© Taosongs TwoHurr
http://www.janisian.com/lyrics/societyschild.php

Hurricane, Bob Dylan and Jacque Levy
© 1975 by Ram's Horn Music; renewed 2003 by Ram's Horn Music
http://bobdylan.com/songs/hurricane/

CAUSE AND EFFECT:

Methamphetamine, Secor and Rawlings
© OCMS ℗ 2008 Nettwerk Productions
https://www.youtube.com/watch?v=Y03JIK3pySs

COMPARISON:

METAPHOR:

A Hard Rain's Gonna Fall, Bob Dylan, © Bob Dylan Music Co.

A Heart of Gold, Neil Young, (p) 1972, Warner Bros Music

Hound Dog, Leiber and Stoller
©Sony/ATV Music Publishing LLC, Warner/Chappell Music, Inc, Universal Music Publishing Group
Love is the Water, Pat Wictor
© Pat Wictor

SIMILE:
Like a Rock, Bob Seeger (1986, © Bob Seger/Capitol Records
Bluest of Things, Carl Cacho,
© 2002, Carl Cacho, Black Holler Music

PROCESS:
**I'm Gonna Make A Cake,* Patty Shukla
© Patty Shukla Kids Music
https://pattyshuklakidsmusic.com/lyrics/
Circle Game, Joni Mitchell (1966)
Sony/ATV Music Publishing LLC, Crazy Crow Music/ Siquomb Music Publishing
Cat's in the Cradle, Harry Chapin, Sandy Chapin
© Warner/Chappell Music, Inc

ARGUMENT:
This Land is Your Land, Woody Guthrie
© T.R.O. Inc. (Public Domain suit pending)
Where Have All the Flowers Gone, Pete Seeger
© Sony/ATV Music Publishing LLC, Universal Music Publishing Group, The Bicycle Music Company
**Plane Wreck at Los Gatos,* Woody Guthrie
© 1961 (renewed) by Woody Guthrie Publications, Inc. & TRO-Ludlow Music, Inc. (BMI)
Lady of the Harbor, Joe Jencks, © Turtle Bear Music/ASCAP

GENERAL:
**It's All Been Done,* Steven Page, ©1998. Warner/Chappell Music, Inc.

SONG AS REFERENCE:
Give Me Your Tired Your Poor (Miss Liberty)
Irving Berlin, Emma Lazarus (1949)
Suzanne, Leonard Cohen, (1966)
© Sony/ATV Music Publishing LLC

IMPORTANCE OF WORDS:
Summertime, George Gershwin/ DuBose Heyward/Ira Gershwin (1935) © Songs Music Publishing
IMPORTANCE OF ACCURACY:
Pride (In the Name of Love), Clayton, Hewson, Mullen, Evans © Universal Music Publishing Group

And the Band Played Waltzing Matilda, Eric Bogle © Peermusic Publishing
The Night They Drove Old Dixie Down, Robbie Roberts, © Warner/Chappell Music, Inc.

ANTHEM:
*#*Which Side Are You On*, Florence Reese (1931) http://unionsong.com/u015.html
**We Shall Overcome, Horton/Carawan/Hamilton/Seeger © The Richmond Organization

*# You can find this song on Google, but it refers to others versions by Billy Bragg and the Dropkick Murphys. The writer, Florence Reese is given credit, however to find the original lyrics in their entirety go to a reputable like unionsong.com.

** The song is most commonly attributed as having descended from "I'll Overcome Some Day", a hymn by Charles Albert Tindley that was first published in 1901. First Modern Version, 1945, and made famous by Joan Baez and Pete Seeger. There is a current battle to release the song into the public domain. This is one song where you can't trust Google. It uses the Joan Baez version, and cites Laurel Aitkin as the songwriter and Sony/ATV as the copyright holder. Most likely, this refers to the version performed by Aitkin.

PART XII: SONGS ON PURPOSE

Before the Fire
Sweet Poison - the fragrance song
Maggie, If You'd Like to Stay
Highway 84
My Daughter
Northern White
Take Care of The Santa Fe
Sweet Amazon
Hey Uncle Tony – the tofu song
Walking Wounded
The Town Called Sugar Grove
The Boy He Used to Be

My songs for a purpose tend to rely heavily on narration and description, however, classification and comparison figure highly as well, and I am carefully to try to convey correct terms via definition. The persuasive mode is evident via pathos, logos, and ethos. I don't have a true "process analysis" song, but may be more likely to convey a sense of "causal analysis."

Before The Fire (Rosewood)

My name is Fannie Taylor and in 1923
I lived next to a sawmill somewhere north of Cedar Key
In the little town of Sumner, divided by race
From the nearby town of Rosewood- such a peaceful place
Before the fire, before the noise.
Before I heard the Sheriff call "Let's go get him boys."
Before the deaths. Before the screams.
I walk the streets of Rosewood in my dreams.
A hundred angry men sent their dogs into the night
To find a black man that they said attacked a woman who was white.
They tortured and they killed and terrorized the town
They took their torches with them and they burned it to the ground.
The Rosewood I remember was a happy place to be.
With 3 churches and two schools, and a baseball team.
Houses always painted, roses everywhere,
And at night piano music filled the air, Before the fire.
    The South it was a hotbed of violence that year
    There were lynchings, there were riots
      Hearts and minds filled with prejudice and fear
      You cannot blame me.
My husband went to work very early every day
And came home very late at night.
I also had a lover who came through my back door
One day he hit me hard with all his might.
To tell the truth about my bruises would have led to my disgrace,
So I said just what came quickest to my tongue
That it was a black man who hit me in the face;
God forgive me I was young.
Before the fire, before the noise.
Before I heard the Sheriff call "Let's go get him boys."
Before the deaths. Before the screams.
I walk the streets of Rosewood in my dreams.
One day it was a place where children went to school
The next I saw it burn before my eyes.
Once upon a time a community with pride,
Before the fire.
Before my lies.

Reason: Song Contest

Primary Purpose: Spread knowledge of this little known historical event

Secondary Purpose: Make people think about the impact events like these had on current racial tensions in our country

Rhetorical Appeals:
Pathos, Ethos

Speaker: Specific non-fictional narrator

Topic: Historical Event

Audience: Most would know very little about this

Details: Used research to be as accurate as possible and to include as many definite descriptions of that time.

Mode: Narrative

Point of View: First Person

Songwriting Conventions: Definite prosody and repeated chorus.

Sweet Poison: The Fragrance Song

He knew she was there when he walked in the room,
He got a whiff of her strong perfume.
A little Chanel, a little Tabu,
He tried to talk but all he could do was
    Achoo!Achoo!Achoo!
He excused himself and went to the loo,
To dab his nose with a soft tissue.
The place was spotless, quite pristine:
Smelled of Pine Sol, and Mr. Clean.
    Achoo!Achoo!Achoo!
We plug it into outlets, spread it on our skins,
Lather up the cleft of a poor man's chin.
Those little pine trees, you've got one or two,
Dangling in your car from your rearview.
Why is it no one thinks, that it's sweet poison –
And that's what stinks.
She was cute when she said all right.
He wanted to say his love was true but
When he kissed her all she could do was
    Achoo! Achoo! Achoo!
Her hair it smelled just like a rose,
His chin it smelled of musk.
When he started to propose
all that they could do was just
    Achoo! Achoo! Achoo!
We plug it into outlets . . .
These lovers made a sacred vow
Now that they're man and wife -
To eliminate those things that smell
That can impact their life
Allergens and phthalates Neurotoxins too,
All synthetic chemicals that just aren't good for you.
Fragrance free they cuddle and dance the hootchie coo
Breathe easily beneath the sheets
But there is one thing they don't do
Achoo, achoo, achoo!
We plug it into outlets . . .
Yeah, it's sweet poison and that's what stinks.

Reason: DJ Angela Page suffers from severe reaction to perfumes. She put out a challenge to songwriters to write about the problem that scent can have for some people.

Primary Purpose: To make people aware that perfumes and other scents can cause allergic reaction.

Secondary Purpose: I couldn't help taking this a step further and talking about the toxic aspects of some scents and perfumes because so many people just aren't aware.

Rhetorical Appeals: This song depends largely on logos – both deductive and inductive reasoning, using examples to draw the conclusion. Pathos is here as well. It appeals to people's desire to be loved and be attractive.

Speaker: Omniscient narrator.

Topic: The dangers of scents and perfumes in our environment.

Audience: General

Tone: Light hearted, slightly comic

Details: There are specific details relating to the perfumes themselves, actually mentioning products. At the moment, these products are still in use. There is also much specific description of the actors and mentions of specific toxins.

Mode: Narrative, Cause and Effect, Description, Illustration, Persuasion

Point of View: Third Person

Songwriting Conventions: Definite verse chorus without a bridge. The chorus is dominant and actually functions as a bridge. This is a wordy song and doubling the verse at the end without the "achoo" in the middle provides a contrast, allows for more words, but is still in keeping melodically. Words like "sweet poison" combined with "That's what stinks" and the interjection of "achoo" keep the listener focused on the topic.

Maggie (If You'd Like to Stay)

I found her on my lawn out in the rain.
Her hair was matted down, she was whimpering in pain.
She was feather light. She was so bone tired
she didn't even notice when I laid her by my fire.

I called her Maggie, yeah Maggie, I don't know where you been.
Maggie, yeah Maggie, looks like you could use a friend,
and if you'd like to stay, you can.

She ate my food but would not let me near.
She growled down in her throat, laid back her ears.
So I gave her space and I gave her time.
One day she wagged her tail - laid her head upon my thigh.

I called her Maggie, yeah Maggie, I don't know where you been.
Maggie, yeah Maggie, looks like you could use a friend,
and if you'd like to stay, you can.

I'd like to find the ones who think it's funny
to chain a dog and leave her starve out in the rain.
I'd like to look 'me in the eye, have a chance to say,
"Did you know she nearly broke her neck, tryin' to get away?"

Every day she babysits my son.
That's a job I don't give to just anyone.
But I know she's bred to guard and take care of
those that need protection, those that give her love.

I called her Maggie, yeah Maggie, I don't know where you been.
Maggie, yeah Maggie, looks like you could use a friend,
And if you'd like to stay,
well, Maggie, oh Maggie, if you'd like to stay, you can.

Reason: I responded to a request by an organization called "Dogs in Chains" to write a song about this issue. The organization never followed up, in fact the outdated web page is still there. It doesn't matter, because contests are always secondary to the song.

Primary Purpose: To call attention to the 2,000 dogs that are kept in chains throughout our country.

Secondary Purpose: To encourage people to rescue dogs in dire straights.

Rhetorical Appeals: There is obviously an overload of pathos in this song. Ethos is established by the singer who rescues a dog in a bad situation. I thought a lot about that bridge. While this song is obviously not meant to change the minds of those who would chain a dog up and leave her to starve, I still didn't want to be too harsh. There is a bit of "do you know" and "are you aware" in this bridge. The narrator would like to be able to talk to these people, but falls short of sending them to the death chamber.

Speaker: Some one who has rescued a dog who has been chained.

Topic: Story of a rescue dog.

Audience: Everyone, especially appealing to those who love animals.

Details: There is a lot of vivid description in this song. Someone told me that "Maggie" is the most common dog name. I used it because my sister-in-law had a dog named Maggie who was a rescue dog that someone had left on their porch. Very often, using real stories to elaborate on allows the writer to be real and fresh.

Mode: Narrative

Point of View: First person

Songwriting Conventions: Verse/Chorus with bridge.

Highway 84

10 miles from Port Jervis, on Highway 84
I can't help remembering' that I've passed this way before.
I drove a boy out to school and drove him back a man.
I can't count the many times I've seen this stretch of land
Chorus
There are those who'll say I could have
spent my time more wisely;
I could have learned something new might of helped
with my success.
I could've given him a car, I could've put him on a plane,
I could've packed up all his stuff,
I could've shipped them both by train.
Instead we folded his long legs and most of his belongings
and filled my white Toyota door to door
and headed out on Highway 84.

We spent the time in talking sharing our philosophies
The world would be a better place left up to him and me.
A comfort when I took wrong turns and yelling at the trucks;
And getting stopped by roadwork and cursing our bad luck
Chorus
In Blacksburg, Virginia today they shake their heads
and try to comprehend why 32 are dead.
A mama sent her babe to school and let go of his hand;
to a quiet and protected place to grow and be a man.
Out of his nest and on his own,
So sad the bird that's barely flown
that's shot down from the sky and never will fly home.
Yes, I might have used that time more wisely.
Done something that was more important I suspect.
But of all the things I'm thankful for, right there on my list,
are those long miles and those short years
I'm glad I didn't miss.
Filling my Toyota door to door and heading off to college,
him and me, and highway 84.

Reason: Personal response to tragedy

Primary Purpose: Personal healing, sympathy for others and thankfulness

Secondary Purpose: Make people relate personally to a tragic event in order to see the importance of protecting our schools and controlling guns in our country.

Rhetorical Appeals:
Pathos, Ethos

Speaker: Self

Topic: Current event

Audience: Most would know a lot about this at the time. A current event this strong will last in our audience's memories for quite awhile.

Details: The general details of the shooting are easy to find in the news. The other details are from personal experience.

Mode: Cause and effect thesis song with the use of narration, illustration, and description.

Point of View: First Person

Songwriting Conventions: Definite prosody and repeated chorus. Use of dramatic shift in tempo for effect.

My Daughter

Nightmares don't come often anymore.
Don't wake up with cold sweats every night.
But I cannot forget the horrors that I met
every murky Mekong Delta morning light.
I know you'll do fine at Fort Jackson –
you're smart and you're strong and you're tough --
but why can't you see what you're doing does to me?
I have had enough.
The jaws of war that lurk beneath the depths of hatred's waters
took away my carefree youth.
Now they want my daughter.

I left you on the sidewalk at the airport --
dropped your bags, slammed my door, and drove away.
And I knew that you were hurt and you were angry.
I'm sorry for the things I couldn't say.
I know that I should stand there by the window
and wave as the plane taxis away,
but I'd put that uniform back on, though it might bleed me dry,
if I could only make you stay.
The war machine that feeds on greed
and serves up senseless slaughter
took away my carefree youth.
Now it wants my daughter.

They stole years from my life. They blew my soul apart.
They ate away my peace of mind -- now they want my heart.
Now, they want my daughter.

I fed you and I clothed you and I worked the daily grind
to show you that I loved you -- never meant to be unkind.
But you don't understand, I can see it in your eyes
why I cannot hold your hand and bid a fond goodbye.
It's just I'm so damned angry – partially at you –
but mostly at this wicked world and the things it wants to do.
Do they have so many bombs and guns they can kill and mess up all
our sons, that they also need my lovely one?
Must they take my daughter?

Reason: Personal

Primary Purpose: To explain to my niece why her Dad was so tough on her when she went to join the army.

Secondary Purpose: To explain the effects of PTSD and convey an anti-war message that includes the military industrial complex.

Rhetorical Appeals: Pathos

Speaker: Non-fictional narrator, not the singer

Topic: Personal story

Audience: Specific on one level, general on another

Details: General knowledge (Viet Nam) Personal knowledge (airport scene, conversation with my niece).

Mode: Narrative, description, persuasion

Point of View: First Person

Songwriting Conventions: Equal narrative verses, short repetitive line in lieu of "chorus" for emphasis, and a bridge to convey the central theme.

Northern White

For 80 years my family's farmed this Wisconsin land,
Now a hydrofracker wants to come and haul away our sand.
Mama said "We're going down to Town Hall today,
To hear what this mining fellow has to say."
    But, you can't eat gas and you can't drink oil
    Mama said that night.
    Businessmen in the clean gray suits,
    Hands all dirty with the northern white.
One 6 second weekly blast," he said, "is all it takes.
You might be surprised how little noise we will make."
But mama said, "Six seconds to foul our air and water,
And take away the future from our sons and daughters."
    You can't eat gas and you can't drink oil
    Mama said that night.
    Businessmen in the clean gray suits,
    Hands all dirty with the northern white.
She turned and saw some friends look away.
Said I can hardly blame you, I know what they will pay.
Farming's hard and sometimes, we cannot meet the bills,
But we should take a lesson from those West Virginia hills
You can't plow gas and you can't plant oil,
can't live on that frac sand.
What will we do after they've gone
and hauled away the land?
Mama's started coughing, sometimes she just can't breathe.
from the gritty chemicals, that this mining leaves.
Between the coughs she tells me, with a rueful laugh,
Write this down my daughter, make it my epitaph:
    You can't eat gas and you can't drink oil
    Mama said that night.
    Businessmen in the clean gray suits,
    Hands all dirty with the northern white.
    Hands all dirty with the northern white.

    Pockets filled with the northern white.

Reason: Song Contest

Purpose: Educate about the lesser know fracking issue of "frack-sand" and make people think about our inter-connectedness and the "one-ness" of the world.

Rhetorical Appeals:
Pathos, Ethos, Logos

Speaker: Un-named fictional narrator

Topic: Current Event

Tone: Serious

Audience: Most would know very little about this

Details: Used research to be as accurate as possible and to include as many definite descriptions of that time. Details came from an article I read about a woman just like the one in the story.

Mode: Narrative

Point of View: First Person

Songwriting Conventions: Definite prosody and repeated chorus. Metaphorical phrase to help people remember the term "Northern White".

Take Care of the Santa Fe

As a child, I fished along her banks -
little cricket on my line -
Hoping for a catch as big as me -
catfish would suit me fine.
My daddy would watch me with a smile
glad to see me play
`longside of the river that he loved.
One day I heard him say

Santa Fe – see her winding, lazy, in the sun.
Santa Fe – feel her giving life to everyone.
She's our legacy. Take care of the Santa Fe for me.

Daddy came to see me in a dream
Said "I am filled with fear.
Something is endangering our river.
I feel it drawing near.
It smells of toxic chemicals and money
and it rumbles underground,
travelin' from its home in Alabama,
Eastward bound.

Santa Fe – see her winding, lazy, in the sun.
Santa Fe – feel her giving life to everyone.
She's our legacy. Take care of the Santa Fe for me.

They say the pipeline's safe,
they call it progress.
But I think we could find
a better way.
We need clean water more than we need methane.
My daddy understood. One day I heard him say

Santa Fe – see her winding, lazy, in the sun.
Santa Fe – feel her giving life to everyone.
She's our legacy. Take care of the Santa Fe for me.

Reason: To enter the Our Santa Fe River Songwriting Competition

Primary Purpose: To write a song that tells a story about the Santa Fe River in Southern Florida.

Secondary Purpose: To convey the importance of the nation's water resources in the face of widespread installation of pipelines to transport fracked gas.

Rhetorical Appeals: Pathos, Ethos, Logos

Speaker: Fictional narrator based on a real person.

Topic: Taken from a current event in the form of a news article.

Audience: Primary: The judges and audience at the competition

Secondary: All audiences

Details: Much was taken from the article. Then I did some research to make sure I had details correct to convey authenticity.

Mode: Narrative

Point of View: First Person

Songwriting Conventions:
The chorus figures prominently because it conveys the importance of the theme. The dramatic melody is meant to stay in people's heads. The chorus also substitutes for the bridge.

Sweet Amazon

Edimar lived in the jungle in a shack by a crystal clear stream.
But now that river is brown with silt and gone is his family's dream
The deer that roamed the land make way for the roads to the mines,
trees are uprooted, and rivulets run cross the forest floor, 40 miles wide.

Take a breath, fill your lungs with that oxygen sensation
Known as air won't be long I fear it might be rationed
If we keep to the perilous path we're on.
I'm really gonna miss you when you're gone – Sweet Amazon.

Kotok is an Indian Living deep within the Amazon
Smoke stings his eyes from the constant fires. His way of life is gone.
And gone are plants for medicine and food.
There's no way to stop it he's afraid,
The white men come, they slash and they burn,
There is just too much money to be made.

We need land to feed the hungry,
We need trees to clean our air.
But soybeans and cattle fill the pockets of the lawless,
and fires are burning everywhere.

Take a breath, fill your lungs with that oxygen sensation
known as air won't be long I fear it might be rationed
If we keep to the perilous path we're on.
I'm really gonna miss you, Really gonna miss you
Really gonna miss you when you're gone - Sweet Amazon.

Reason: I responded to an article I read in a magazine. I am always interested in environmental issues.

Primary Purpose: To tell the story of Edimar, his family, and their predicament.

Secondary Purpose: To bring to light to the importance of the Amazon region as the "lungs" of our world and the dire consequences of its slow demise.

Rhetorical Appeals: There is actually a bit of logos in this song. Deductive reasoning is used to describe the potential long-term disaster of ruining the rain forest. Since this is a real story, Ethos is there in the background, while pathos underlies Kotok's predicament.

Speaker: Omniscient narrator.

Topic: Damage being done to the rainforest

Audience: General

Details: There is a lot of description in this song with the attempt to portray vividly what is happening. The details are taken from the article and therefore, are able to be substantiated.

Mode: Narrative

Point of View: Third Person

Songwriting Conventions: This is a fairly short song with just two verses, two choruses, a bridge and a little coda. Generally tight and well-crafted.

Hey Uncle Tony (The Tofu Song)

Hey Uncle Tony, Go to lunch with me
Veggie Kitchen is the place I'd like to me
Try a little tofu, what do you say?
He said, A little bit of tofu goes a long way
A little bit of tofu goes a long way.

(Chorus): Hand me the sirloin and the apple pie;
Chicken fried. Potatoes mashed.
White bread and butter and lots of jam,
Don't you forget the corned beef hash.
Don't you forget the corned beef hash.

Hey Uncle Tony, here's some brown rice.
Its good for you and it sure tastes nice.
Tony took a forkful, turned to say
A little bit of brown rice goes a long way.
A little bit of brown rice goes a long way. (Chorus)

Hey Uncle Tony, here's some bean sprout,
Full of lots of good things without a doubt.
Tony ate just one, put the rest away,
Said a little bit of bean sprout goes a long way
A little bit of bean sprout goes a long way. (Chorus)

Hey uncle Tony I'm afraid you'll die
If you keep on eating this way
He said everybody's gotta go sometime
I'm gonna go with a smile on my face
I'm gonna go with a smile on my face. (Chorus)

Hey uncle Tony, gonna have the last laugh
Cause I'm gonna write your epitaph
He would still be here today
If he hadn't pushed the tofu away.

So go easy on the sirloin and the apple pie,
Add a little celery and walnuts and greens,
Don't eat quite as much chicken and spuds
Throw in blueberries and almonds and beans.
A little bit of tofu goes along way
And I want you there on my wedding day.
I want you there on my wedding day.

Reason: Song challenge – I don't even remember the theme suggestion! I think we were supposed to use a person's name. I was at a health food restaurant with a friend, and the song was a done deal!

Primary Purpose: To write a song in a day, given a particular song prompt.

Secondary Purpose: Illustrate the importance of healthy eating.

Rhetorical Appeals: Cause and Effect, Persuasion, Humor

Speaker: First Person fictional narrator

Topic: Healthy Eating, general

Audience: Everyone – I made a particular point at the end to not be didactic. There is not one way to healthy eating and the foods that Uncle Tony like are terrible – only one should have a varied diet and think "include" rather than exclude. The ending helps to achieve my purpose by not alienating the audience, but giving them something to think about.

Details: Drawn from typical "health" foods

Mode: Narrative

Point of View: First Person

Songwriting Conventions: The a cappella "rap-like" nature is meant to create a fun tone. The chorus, which does not echo the point of the song, but rather the anti thesis takes up a good portion of the song. I have created another version that groups the verses together and has fewer choruses. It is better for getting the meaning across, but not as entertaining for the audience, since the chorus exemplifies much of the flavor of "Uncle Tony".

Walking Wounded

Here's to the walking wounded caught up in some purgatory place,
Void of time and space, longing for rebirth as they wander on this earth.

A bomb goes off in Bagdad and nothing's left of someone's baby boy.
A folded flag in his mama's hands, as his daddy stands
his shoulders shake as he tries to forget the pain
and remember all the joy.
Somehow they'll manage to go on
but with every breath they take they will always know
a part of them is gone.
Chorus:

> *And there' s a hobo in an alleyway,*
> *asleep beneath the front-page news.*
> *Target of the pelting rain,*
> *wearing someone else's worn out shoes*
> *And hope is what is left inside*
> *some kid's discarded Dixie Cup.*
> *You swallow it like wounded pride,*
> *so hungrily you suck it up.*

Though it's only 10 am her hand's around
a half gone bottle of Tanqueray Gin.
Some how it seems to ease the pain, the day the planes
brought down the towers on that September morning --
that's where it began.
She still hears the crying through the haze
And she sits there in a daze because she'll always know
some of her faith is gone.
Chorus
For 60 years right by his side from the day
she said she'd be his bride
To the day they put her in the ground
And he knows that she won't be around.
Sometimes it makes him want to cry.
Somehow he knows that he'll go on
But the days and nights are long when the only one you've loved
Forever will be gone.
Here's --- to the walking wounded.

Reason: I was invited to write a song for an ADAA (Anxiety and Depression Association of America) support group.

Primary Purpose: It was after my mother passed in 2012. That aspect, plus the ongoing trauma of 9/11 and the Iraq war worked their way into this song about those trying to survive loss.

Secondary Purpose: To draw a general picture of those who go through life after being affected by loss. Often their sadness not actually quantified as depression, but still strong enough to impact their lives forever.

Rhetorical Appeals: Pathos, Ethos

Speaker: Third person

Topic: Emotional Loss

Audience: Primary: ADAA, Secondary: All audiences

Details: I tried to use descriptive details that are effective and appropriate. They convey to the audience what has happened and the specificity adds to the realism.

Mode: Narrative, Description, Illustration,

Point of View: Omniscient

Songwriting Conventions:
The song is a 'circular' song, beginning and ending with a significant phrase that functions as a bridge might. It consists of three equal verses illustrating three separate cases. The chorus is a metaphor and is another example of the primary metaphor, "walking wounded." The chorus has a different rhythm and feel to the verses; the technique is used deliberately to hopefully draw a line between this metaphor and the illustrations.

The Town of Sugar Grove

Leave at night when the wind is still
Leave when the clouds are hanging low.
I hear you can find safe harbor
In the town of Sugar Grove – Sugar Grove

At the end of Big Tree Road sits a woman at her door
She is sewing freedom clothes, her fingers they are strong and sure.
Comes a knocking in the night - a fugitive from slavery
trembling in the icy cold. "Oh mistress, have pity on me"
"Doctor, doctor"! she cried. "Help me save this dying soul
And we will put him back on the road to freedom
After we have made him whole."

Leave at night when the wind is still
Leave when the clouds are hanging low.
I hear you can find safe harbor
In the town of Sugar Grove – Sugar Grove

There within her Mansion fine The Ladies Fugitive Society
Meets each week to sew for those who would be free.
There within her Mansion Fine she serves Frederick Douglas tea
He says 'Thank you madam for your aid in time of need.
Here in Sugar Grove we can make the whole world see
There is no North, South, East or West
There is only equality

In the town of Sugar Grove across the Pennsylvania hills
Is a woman you should know, brave of heart and strong of will

Go to Sugar Grove quietly before the dawn.
You may find she's waiting for her patiently waiting.
Giving strength to carry on.

Leave at night when the wind is still
Leave when the clouds are hanging low.
I hear you can find safe harbor
In the town of Sugar Grove
Ask for Cynthia Catlin Miller in the town called Sugar Grove.

Reason: I wanted to write a song and enter it in The Pennsylvania Heritage Songwriting Competition.

Primary Purpose: To relate in an interesting manner, the story of this fascinating woman and the town called Sugar Grove. Context: Pennsylvania connection

Secondary Purpose: To educate people about this little known element of Pennsylvania History and an important chapter in Civil Rights history.

Rhetorical Appeals: Pathos, Ethos,

Speaker: Omniscient

Topic: Historical. The song recounts the true story of abolitionist activist Cynthia Catlin Miller who lived in the town of Sugar Grove, Pennsylvania.

Tone: Serious; conveyed by rhythm and melody:
Meant to convey the urgency of nighttime flight of those who needed help and protection.

Audience: Ostensibly the selection committee of the competition. More universally, all audiences who would benefit from learning this fascinating and under known story.

Details: The details of an historical narrative should be as accurate as research can make it. Such details in this song are:

- The name of the town
- Cynthia Catlin Miller was very real. She came from a wealthy family and ran a sewing group in her home that made clothes for the escaped slaves that came through Sugar Grove on their way to cross over into Canada.
- The Millers lived on Big Tree Road
- One night a fugitive slave arrived at her door and she called her sister, a doctor, to come and tend him.
- Frederick Douglas did come to speak in Sugar Grove and I used a phrase from his speech there: "There is no north, south, east or west, only equality."

- The slaves would travel by night
- Again I wanted to be consistent with this being about Cynthia and eliminate the mild and repetitive. Although I liked the Cherry Hill reference, there was some confusion among listeners because of the tense shift – plus there is no history of ghosts around the cemetery – though she helped in the abolitionist movement, there is no real evidence she hid a lot of slaves and I wouldn't want to give that feeling. She organized things, and was a staunch opponent of slavery – the one story about the slave who came to her door is true, but I didn't want to stretch it beyond belief.

Mode: Narrative

Point of View: Omniscient

The Boy He Used to Be

Cheeks like apples; a great big laugh,
a wholesome, happy lad.
They dressed him up, gave him a gun,
sent him out to face a world gone mad.
Did what he was told to do, then quietly came home.
Left behind a shattered youth in the trenches of Toulon.

Oh he did not speak about it; he could not let them see
that he would never be the same – the boy he used to be.

As a child when kids were cruel,
he would not fight them after school.
He would turn the other cheek –
believed that golden rule.
When death was his companion it tore him up inside--
The grim and ugly deeds of war he did just to survive.

Oh he did not speak about it and he could not let them see
that he would never be the same, the boy he used to be.

Went to church, knelt to pray, read his Bible faithfully each day.
Raised a family, worked a job,
seemed to get along ok.
Somewhere through the years, his prayers ran out of breath
And this godly man slowly drank himself to death.

Oh he did not speak about it and he could not let them see
that he would never be the same, the boy he used to be.

These lyrics are used to illustrate Cause and Effect, p. 85.

PART XIII: WRITING TIPS EDITING CONTESTS

Meaning and prosody

"Rhymes are one of the most important tools you have in your toolbox when writing a song. If a song is like a sentence, rhyme is the punctuation: the periods and commas of a song. It creates moments where we hear sonic connections between words, so we stop and notice what's going on. It's a highlighting tool that can be used to support the meaning of your lyrics. What you choose to rhyme and which kinds of rhyme you use will change how the listener feels when he or she hears your song."

~Susan Cattaneo, Berklee College of Music
http://americansongwriter.com/2014/02/susan-cattaneos-songwriting-course-rhyme-reason/

Prosody:

Prosody simply means that the words and music go together. The stresses of the words fit the musical pattern of the song. In addition, some use prosody to define the way melody, chords, and meter exemplify the song's meaning.

Rhyme and Prosody are your friends. Some people like to use rhyming dictionaries. These can be helpful, but limit your use of them. Sometimes searching for that right rhyme can shake things up a bit; you might end up changing the word you are trying to rhyme with, and that creates new ideas.

Prosody can be stretched a bit if it helps meaning, but searching for the perfect set of lyrics that also fits perfectly into your meter can be a good challenge for getting your message across.

You will always find that you will be tempted to veer from exact prosody and rhyme in order to accomplish your purpose. Don't be afraid of "near" rhymes if it is better for your meaning. Many songs today are filled with "near" rhymes, which perhaps only have the vowel sound in common. The listener's ear is not so discriminating that it picks up on this, and since they are so common in contemporary music, no one is going to criticize their use. The most important thing is achieving the meaning you want. If you can get a perfect rhyme that fits smoothly and achieves your meaning, that is great. But, if not, it is ok to go with close. Since the purpose is a primary goal, sometimes this is allowable and actually works well. However, it is important to remember that the song conventions that have been around for hundreds of years are there for a reason. They are easy on the ears of the audience.

As you edit, work hard to combine both the writing conventions that make listening easy with your desire to convey your purpose.

Editing:

> *"Kill your darlings, kill your darlings, even when it breaks your egocentric little scribbler's heart, kill your darlings."*
> ~ Stephen King, On Writing: A Memoir of the Craft

> *"Put down everything that comes into your head and then you're a writer. But an author is one who can judge his own stuff's worth, without pity, and destroy most of it."*
> ~ Colette, Casual Chance

Wow. "Breaks your heart". "Judge". "Destroy". These seem like harsh words. Yes, editing is very tough, but sometimes if we are honest we can do a lot of personal editing. I have heard good songs that their writers claim were not edited – that they just came to them in one piece. I do believe this can happen, but it is rare. Even if you write pretty good first drafts, all songs need to be looked over and reviewed. Some of this editing might have to do with your "purpose."

I have also heard many songwriters say that we always love that current song we are working on. It is always the best and we are very eager to get it out into the world. Sometimes, we are too eager to do just that.

All editing, be it for a novel, a film or a song, has things in common. However, each requires some specific tools. In songwriting, we are editing for several things including prosody, meaning, and music.

Editing for lyrical meaning

Purpose-filled songs are the most difficult to write. Remember that first we must think about our audience. That is why it is important to edit for their benefit. Sometimes things that are clear to us are not as clear as we think they are to everyone. One way to edit for the audience is simply to try the song out at open mikes or for family and friends. Don't preface the song, simply sing it and pay attention to the reaction. If you begin to hear feedback that is not what you intended, take another look at the song.

Another way to edit for meaning when you think you really have a good first draft is to find a really good set of ears. This can take place a songwriting camp, or with in a professional mentoring session; however, you can also just find someone whose judgment you trust to give the song a listen and give you feedback on meaning.

It is important to point out, to those who fear peer editing because they don't like "criticism", is that this isn't a dirty word. One definition of the word will tell you that it is "the expression of disapproval of someone or something based on perceived faults or mistakes". Sounds very negative doesn't it? However, the second definition of criticism is "the analysis and judgment of the merits and faults of a literary or artistic work." Synonyms are evaluation, assessment, and analysis.

Good writing is good editing, and sometimes we cannot be good editor because our sense of objectivity is compromised. In this case, we need to go to a professional or peer for evaluation and suggestions.

Peer Editing:

The job of your peer is to just tell you what they heard. If what they heard is not what you intended, then it is time to edit. Ask your listener what he/she heard. Don't explain your song unless asked to do so, after you have heard this feedback. This process can sometimes take several listens. In the end, after several drafts and several sets of ears, you will choose which edits you feel are important and make those changes. Sometimes, especially in songwriting groups where people are looking at your lyrics, critiques can be too focused and go way beyond what the normal person is going to hear. In these instances, you may choose to keep it the way you had it originally.

Editing for Structure:

Once you feel that the basic meaning is evident, you need to go through and edit the song so that the structure is as precise as possible. Find those rhymes that don't quite work; eliminate unnecessary words looking particularly at situations where you are trying to fit too many words into a measure or where you include throwaway articles or adjectives that might not be necessary. Think about whether you need that extra chorus and check to make sure that stanzas are equally written.

Editing for melody and chord progressions

Sing the song to yourself enough to get a sense for whether the melody is working. Does the melody and chord progression match the mood of the song? Are you singing the melody the same in every chorus? Does the melody of the chorus differ enough from the melody in the verse? Does the chord progression modulate well from the verse into the bridge and back again?

There are some great books that have been written about editing for prosody and for musical reasons. What I have pointed out are some some simple suggestions. Check out my

Resources section for sources that will help you with these types of edits.

A Personal Editing Session with a Pro:

I think that I am capable of writing a pretty good song on the first try, and doing it quickly. However, I have never written one that didn't need some editing. One of the things I do with a song I am not sure of, is to sign up for a web-critique with a pro. Currently I have been going to Jason Blume, a well-known and highly regarded Nashville-based songwriter. Now, Jason is not a writer of socially conscious, purposeful folk songs. He tends to personally be focused on the commercial market. However, Jason has an uncanny knack for hearing what is good in any song, and for providing thought-provoking insight into meaning, melody, and prosody. He's a great second set of ears.

Let me tell you about a couple of songs I took to Jason. The first song is called *Leaving Atlanta.*

Here is the first set of lyrics:

Leaving Atlanta

Could the sun be any brighter on such a dismal day?
Could you hold me any tighter now that I'm going away?
There are many things I know, deep down in my soul
But I don't know why I'm leaving Atlanta.

Could it be more amusing that I am filled with fear
That what seems to be confusing is really very clear.
There are many things I know, deep down in my soul
But I don't know why I'm leaving Atlanta.

Bridge: You say I run whenever things get hard.
You look into my eyes and tell me you see scars

Well maybe it's so. But all that I know
Is I'm leaving Atlanta.

I know every storm is not a hurricane.
And I know that the thunder comes before the rain.
There are many things I know
Deep down in my soul.
But I don't know why I'm leaving Atlanta.

It might turn out ok, should I decide to stay.
But I guess we'll never know – oh –
Because I'm leaving Atlanta.

Jason's first comment was, that while he often likes ambiguity, there was some ambiguity in these lyrics that just wasn't working for him. He said he was left feeling that "of course she knows why she is leaving." This echoed my own skepticism about the first two lines of the second verse and the last quatrain. I had written the song very quickly as part of "FAWM" (February Album Writing Month) and was focused mostly on prosody – I wanted to get something out there that fit.

Those first two lines of the second verse are saying, "isn't it funny that afraid that I will find out that I am not confused at all and that I really do know why I am leaving." That really doesn't make much sense.

Another point he made was about the coda. The language seemed awkward to him and he thought it would be better if it were phrased, "if I decided to stay." In reviewing that, I felt I knew what was bothering him: it was the perfect tense. While "decided" was not going to work well rhythmically, I felt I could achieve the same feeling by changing "should decide" to "did decide" to stay. Grammatically, that is more accurate and closer to "decided" – in fact, it is more grammatically correct.

He mentioned that in the bridge, he felt "leaving Atlanta" was repetitive and he would like to hear something fresh there.

Finally, he was left a bit dazed by the reference to the things the singer did know: "every storm is not a hurricane", and "the thunder comes before the rain". In musing on this phrase, he said he thought the perhaps these were metaphors for relationships? He wondered if what I was saying was that all small problems are not big ones and that sometimes what seems to be a problem is soothed later? Although he did not seem too certain about this, nor was I sure he liked that explanation, it ironically was exactly what I had intended. So, because he (with his good set of ears) heard what I intended, I decided to keep that. In any event, they are cool metaphors!

Jason made a couple of great observations about my melody. There was something about it that wasn't reaching him, but he couldn't put a finger on it. Again, the good set of ears hears, and it is up to me, the writer, to reflect on that. What I realized upon examination is that the melody depended largely on descending and ascending runs. Both the melody and chorus were composed of 4 notes in succession. There wasn't enough variety in the melodic style. To remedy this, I changed the verse melody to one that went "back and forth" instead of in stair steps.

Another comment he made was that the small chorus, or what is really a refrain, was not ending on the tonic chord and that he was longing to hear it resolved. I had left it unresolved intentionally, thinking it added interest, but on reflection, I realized that he was right – the ear wants to hear that resolved.

This is the second set of lyrics:

Could the sun be any brighter on such a dismal day?
Could you hold me any tighter now that I'm going away?
There are many things I know, deep down in my soul
But I don't know why I'm leaving Atlanta.

Could it be more confusing, this eagerness and fear?
This wanting to be leaving, while holding back the tears?
There are many things I know, deep down in my soul
But I don't know why I'm leaving Atlanta.

You say I run whenever things get hard.
You look into my eyes and tell me you see scars
Well maybe it's so, but all that I know
is I have to go. (resolve melody)

I know every storm is not a hurricane.
And I know that the thunder comes before the rain.
There are many things I know deep down in my soul.
But I don't know why I'm leaving Atlanta.

It might turn out ok, if I **did decide** to stay.
But I guess we'll know – oh –
Because I'm leaving Atlanta.

I was happy with all of the edits, and because of those tweaks, I now had a much stronger song that was less ambiguous, but still had intrigue.

If this session seems as if Jason was only pointing out the negatives of this song, I need to emphasize that he is always respectful. There is no such thing as being thin-skinned in the music business. He encouraged me to continue working on the song because it was worthwhile. It is Jason's professional candor that makes me trust him when he points out the things he feels are strong within a song as well as those he thinks are weak.

When I took him my second song he said, "I won't have much to say about this song." That, of course, was gratifying, as was the positive reaction from several of the online participants. However ... there is always something.

Here are the original lyrics:

Sailor on a Lost Ocean

I've never been in love
I liked to be alone
Didn't need nobody.

I could make it on my own.
Then I saw you there
I was in love at the start
But I just don't know
How to win your heart.
I'm a sailor on a lost ocean,
Skydiver in a stormy sky.
Cowboy without a saddle, am I.
I told my friend
I don't know what to do.
I'm so in love.
I haven't got a clue
Cause I've never been
In love before.
It's a problem
I can't ignore
I'm a sailor on a lost ocean,
Skydiver in a stormy sky.
Cowboy without a saddle, am I.
Oh pretty baby
Won't you give me a sign
Is there anyway
That I can make you mine?
I am a drifting
Boat without a sail
Knight without an armor,
Hammer without a nail.
I'm a sailor on a lost ocean,
Skydiver in a stormy sky.
Cowboy without a saddle, am I
I'm a sailor on a lost ocean,
Skydiver in a stormy sky.
Cowboy without a saddle-
Up the creek without a paddle,
Fighting a losing battle, am I.

This is basically a pop song that I wrote to the song-writing prompt "lost ocean". Jason first indicated that he thought maybe saying "a sailor lost upon an ocean" would make more sense. However, he felt that given the genre of the song, the audience would not be bothered by it.

His next comment had to do with word choice. He then wondered if maybe "anyone" instead of "nobody" might be better in the first verse.

His only other comment had to do with the second verse. It seemed generic and repetitive. Other than those things, he loved the song, didn't dislike the use of the clichés at the end and had no comments about the melody.

I was glad he wasn't too bothered by the "lost ocean" bit, because that is exactly what I meant. In my mind, the singer is navigating uncharted waters. The singer isn't lost, but rather sailing someplace she has never been before; in effect, it was lost to her. He liked the effect of the language and was very happy to keep it even if some listeners might scratch their heads about it. I hoped that the use of the other metaphors (skydiver in a stormy sky etc.) made it work.

He was definitely correct about the second verse. I had thrown in some general lines to finish the song in time (if was for a "song-a-day for a week" challenge) and it doesn't add any thing. So I decided to change that verse, make it more concrete, and in keeping with the "sailor" theme. I changed "nobody" to "anyone" because I could make it fit, and rewrote the second verse:

> I watch the sun rise, on a sea so blue.
> I spent all night, thinking 'bout you.
> A wave of longing floods my soul
> And I get feelings I can't control.

I am much happier with that verse now. It has lyrical substance through the use of metaphor and adds to the mood, and is more concrete.

What I like about going to someone like Jason, is that I know I am taking my song to a very educated set of ears. He has heard thousands of songs. As a discerning writer, I don't always change things he comments on and he doesn't insist upon particular changes. Rather, he calls on the writer to listen again, and to make sure that what we are saying is what we are really meaning to say. To learn more about Jason and about some other songwriting critique possibilities, check out my Resources section.

Example of a self-edit via a peer comment:

I wrote fourteen songs in the month of February for an activity called February Album Writing Month (FAWM). I was in Georgia and the weather had been good, but on the second day of the song challenge, it began to rain. Feeding off of that and from some personal grief, I wrote a song called "Rainy Day in Georgia. "When I posted it, someone commented that they liked the song, but it had "lots of words." Ha! That's me.

So, I looked closely and found those places where the words weren't necessary to convey the meaning. The song was originally 4:26 minutes long without any instrumentals. After the edit, it was 3:16. The length of a song is not a goal in itself, but I personally feely that stories can be told effectively in under four minutes, which demands less of the audience's attention. With the shorter time period, I could include an intro and instrumental bridge in performance. Below is the song, with the simple edits I made – they mostly consist of just removing text that is not needed:

FAWM #2: Rainy Day in Georgia

~~The sun was soft as angel hair~~
~~As I was walking yesterday.~~
~~I bought a dozen coffees~~
~~And I gave them all away~~
~~to the homeless men who slept against the wall.~~
~~As~~ I gave ~~one~~ a coffee (to a homeless man)
(and) He said well thank you ma'am.
I said 'you happy for sunshine?"

He said you bet I am.
with a toothless grin if I recall.
But the sun has turned to rain
And he is keeping dry somewhere
With a paper bag that's filled with wine.
It's a rainy day in Georgia
And that suits me just fine.
I'm feeling kind of guilty
I've got shelter, I've got food.
But a sunny day was wrong for me
I'm more in the mood
For a day that's stormy
and for skies of gray.
~~I listen to the patter of~~
~~The raindrops in the wind~~
~~And I'm happy for the sound~~
~~And for the feeling on my skin~~
~~that's a little like my heart feels today.~~
You used to love that sunshine
And why you are gone
Is something I have never understood
It's a rainy day in Georgia
And a little rain just does me good.
~~I know that you told me~~
~~It was just your time to go~~
~~And that sometimes there is~~
~~Nothing we can do – I know~~
~~And I am trying hard to believe~~
(I know) That ~~you and I~~ (we) will meet again
Just like I learned in Sunday School
We will hug again as friends
And that day is coming soon.
Meanwhile it's OK for me to grieve
So I don't mind at all.
Those little drops of pain
can soothe a soul that bleeds.

It's a rainy day in Georgia
And a little rain is what I need.

Sometimes, just a little self-editing is all that we need. Cut away the deadwood and write a song that is clean and concise and says just what is necessary. A simply comment by a peer can get it started.

Contests

People often ask me about contests. It is said that songwriting is not a competitive sport. One venue operator posed the question as to why people expend their energies on competitions that aren't, in her case anyway, making them more marketable as performers.

I can only answer these questions as they apply to me. There is competition in everything, and attitude and expectations when involved in contests is key to how much you will gain in participating in such events.

I have won, placed or been a finalist in 24 contests over the last few years. Sometimes these contests are local affairs, sponsored by state or regional groups, and often they include writing on a theme. Some have required that I travel and participate in the competition, while others have told me I have won and sent me a check.

I have never entered The John Lennon Songwriting Competition, the International Songwriting Competition, or the USA Songwriting Competition. The reason for that is simply that these contests give awards but do not allow for a performance opportunity.

My goal in entering contests, is to expand my reach and spread my music around. Songwriting contests that require performance allow me to do that. Because writing on demand and on a theme is a strength of mine (often using the modes of development), I find these latter types stimulating from a writing standpoint as well. Even if I did not win, I often came out with a new song that was, as we say, a "keeper".

There are basically two types of songwriting competitions: Performing and non-performing. Non-performing contests announce awards, send out the prizes, and the artist can then post their success on social media.

Performing song contests can operate in one of two ways. In one case, the writer is informed that he/she has won or placed in the contest and that their prize is in the mail. At that point, the writer is "greatly encouraged" to come and play the song at the sponsoring festival.

In other circumstances, the writer is announced that he/she is a finalist and must come to the festival to compete for one of the top honors.

Both styles have their advantages. Obviously, knowing that you have won the contest and have prize money in hand is awesome. You can go to the contest feeling relaxed. Going as a finalist however, hones the performance chops. The downside to open contests is that you must decide whether spending the money to go to one of these contests is worth it, in the event that you do not win anything. Also, it is more difficult for an outsider to win or place at some local contests. There is often an understandable local bias from the judges.

Example: I received the email from the Woody Guthrie Festival that I had won first place and my check for $500 was in the mail. Would I be coming to play they asked? Sure, says I! Great, says they. You get to open the big, last night of the festival on the Pastures Of Plenty stage with a thirty-minute set. Sounds good to me, I said. I went to Oklahoma City, and visited this place I had never been before. Since I had a cousin near Tulsa, I had added incentive to go to Oklahoma. In addition, I was able to take the trip down old Route 66, a road my dad had traveled from Arkansas to California as a kid during the Great Depression. The festival was a blast, with other performing opportunities on an open mike stage, and provided just a great time to wander around and listen. This was definitely worth the trip, as I made connections, sold CD's etc.

Another first place win, to the Will McLean Festival in Florida was worth going as well. I remember that I kept getting calls to my phone that I didn't get to in time. Finally, there was a voice message on my machine. "Is this Jane Fallon? Well you are the winner in our contest," said the voice with a definite Southern drawl. "What can we do to get you here? We will give you $300, we will put you up, we will pick you up." Well, how could I say no, especially since I have a son in Tampa whom I could visit. It was a great time. The audience was very receptive and my worries that some might not welcome a Northerner coming into their state and relating an unsavory part of their history. Quite to the contrary - most were very grateful and appreciative that I would tell the story of Rosewood so that the rest of the world could hear it. This is a "folk" community after all, and it's namesake, Will McLean, was a folk troubadour who did not shy from singing about justice.

So, in these cases it was definitely worth the trips, even if they ate into my profits.

Some songwriting opportunities allowed me emotional satisfaction. In 2012, my father passed away. He was a cattle rancher from Oregon, but he died when visiting me in New Hampshire. One thing I held on to, before shipping him back West, was his cowboy hat. I entered a song I had written about him, called *He Deserves The Hat,* and submitted it to a songwriting competition at Neuse River Music Festival held at Lenoir College in South Carolina. When they called to say I had won second, I packed up the hat and took off. I needed that independent journey to reflect. I stopped at places I had never been, I struck up conversations with bartenders, and I followed Rhonda Vincent and the Range onto the main stage and was able to do three songs. Again, I met people, expanded my horizons, and handed out business cards. This event yielded a house concert the next year and I had a great time. I came home feeling as if I had paid homage to my dad, and that he would have gotten a kick out of it.

The most competitive and subjective of all contests is the one in which you must go to the location and perform for judges. Usually there are three to ten finalists. If you don't win, you usually end up with nothing. I have yet to win first as a finalist in a performance, however, these are also beneficial.

In several instances, I placed, which is great. I consider any event where I place and I am an out-of-area person, to be a great win. These contests took me as well, to places I had never been. I won second in the Ozark Music Festival, located in the quaint and interesting town of Hot Springs, AR. What I remember about that competition was stopping some folks in their tracks with my song *A Capella Ella* – (one more piece of evidence as to the power of the human voice). Though I didn't win, I felt valued, met some new friends, and saw a new place.

Another contest took me to LaCrosse, WI. I came in second there, but with many members of the audience telling me I was their choice for first. There was a wonderful moment when I looked out at an audience where I knew no one, and heard the silence fall as I opened my mouth. I sensed them questioning, "Who is this woman?" I saw the smiles and appreciated their appreciation. Meanwhile, I really enjoyed La Crosse, spent some time in Madison and got to visit Taliesin East (I am a big Frank Lloyd Wright Fan) and especially enjoyed my leisurely drive down the Mississippi River – who knew it was way up there?

I had a friend who said once that songwriting contests are a crapshoot. There is a certain truth to that. How one fares in a songwriting contest is filled with "depends." Sometimes contests are looking for specific topics. Sometimes they are looking for specific styles. I can't be sure, but sometimes despite saying that the arrangement doesn't matter, it can't help but sway the judges when a song is performed well. I think that in the case of contests where there are 1000's of entries, the "crapshoot" factor is bigger than one where there are 50 entries.

For instance, I wrote *Northern White* for a Song Of The Month competition for a specific organization. I did not get one of the top three prizes in that competition, but I saw value in this song. I felt the topic was strong, the purpose well-formed, and the hook and chorus were compelling. And so I sent it into the Woody Guthrie Songwriting Competition and won first place. When I talked to someone there about the song a man said, "We were looking for songs about fracking. We got a lot on that topic but yours was the best written." Later, I sent in a few songs to an environmental songwriting competition, and they chose this song as the Grand Prize Winner. The lesson here is to learn what a "good" song is. That is the first requirement. Remember what I said earlier about not letting one rejection get you down – if you feel you have a good song, don't give up on it.

Songwriting competitions can be subjective. They are affected by personal preferences and cultural concerns. In the case of *Northern White,* the judges were attracted to hard-hitting songs that dealt directly with hydro-fracking. However, in Oklahoma where fracking has had a major impact, they made the connection between sand mining in Wisconsin and how it helped to dig out the shale in Oklahoma. I could have written a great song about something else, but not won. The timing of the song and the location of the contest were important. But most importantly – it was a well-written song.

If entering and succeeding in competitions is your "purpose", then do the research. Make sure you understand what "genre" of songs the competition is looking for. Listen to what has won in the past if possible. I was told that one artist says he listens to what won in the past, and then writes a song just like it. However, that won't work for every one. I usually pick something from my stash of songs that is similar in feel. Even then, I find that choices can vary from year to year. Send your best songs.

Don't get down if you are not selected. Understand that a lot of very good material is being submitted. Check your budget and decide if your chance of being a finalist is worth the entry fee, if there is one.

Entering contests is just one way to hone your skills and challenge your ability to write for a "purpose." Let's face it, we live in a world where perception matters and in getting others to talk about our writing is key. Accolades such as contests help in creating that perception and in getting our great songs out there!

PART XIV: SUMMARY

Well, first of all, I don't consider it a craft. I consider it poetry and art. Craftsmanship, when it comes to songwriting, I find kind of offensive.

~ Guy Clark

Somebody said to me, but the Beatles were anti-materialistic. That's a huge myth. John and I literally used to sit down and say, Now, let's write a swimming pool.

~Paul McCartney

My best songs were written very quickly. Just about as much time as it takes to write it down is about as long as it takes to write it...

~Bob Dylan

Out of my entire annual output of songs, perhaps two, or at the most three, came as a result of inspiration. We can never rely on inspiration. When we most want it, it does not come."

~George Gershwin

"I wake up from dreams and go, 'Wow, put this down on paper.' The whole thing is strange. You hear the words, everything is right there in front of your face."

~Michael Jackson

"Songwriting is a very mysterious process. It feels like creating something from nothing. It's something I don't feel like I really control."

~Tracy Chapman

"It's my responsibility as a singer/songwriter to report the news."

~John Mellencamp

Yes, there are as many ways to go about this songwriting thing as there are songwriters. Is it art? Is it inspiration? Is it a craft? Is it a mystical alchemy? It is all of those things and more. It is difficult to see the poetic arts in the same light as the more concrete forms, but the ancient Greeks proved that we humans have a need to assign form to the intangible.

You might be saying at the end of this book, "What? I should THINK about my songs? Doesn't that take away from the feel? Doesn't that diminish emotion? I will say, "Not at all." The brain influences your emotions through special neurons.

We are all one piece. Not only is the foot bone connected to the anklebone, but also the eyes and ears pull on the heart-strings, and the mind controls it all. We can debate whether or not songwriting is an art, a craft, or simple inspiration, but really good art causes people to think.

> *Art causes people to look a little closer. To look closer at the social issues, at other people and their emotions, at the environment that surround them, and the everyday objects and life forms around them. It helps them see what is there but not easily perceived. The artist brings out that which cannot be seen or felt easily.*
>
> *When society sees and feels clearly on these things, it provides opportunities for change in thought or appreciation of the message behind the art. It can cause people to re-examine their thinking on the subject that's put before them.*
>
> ~Brian Rice, Canadian Painter
> www.rosendaleschoolofarts.com

To achieve this requires effort. All writing is process. Sometimes it seems as if your song comes to you, springing forward in one piece like Athena from the brow of Zeus. However, according to the myth, Zeus swallowed Athena's pregnant mother because of a prophecy that she would bear a child to over-throw him. So, even Athena did not really come from nothing. Your previous knowledge of songwriting techniques, and your innate understanding of the modes of development, often shape songs that seem to come easy. Even in those instances, you will find yourself changing a word here or there to be more precise, editing for length, or tweaking a boring melody.

If you want to use songwriting as a means of catharsis, and you don't really care if the audience understands it all, then ignore this entire book. However, if you have a particular meaning you want to get across, think more deeply. We don't always like to do it, but it can be highly rewarding.

It is always important to remember that tools are just tools. They do not replace inspiration, but they are there to help you focus that inspiration. You can't find the elephant inside the slab of marble until you start whittling away at it.

I am going to end this book with an exercise. One semester, for a class in argumentative writing, I suggested that each student pick a topic. From this topic they would craft four separate papers over the course of the semester. This confused them slightly. How can one write four papers on one topic? It wasn't long before they learned that a topic is not a thesis.

So let's do that here, using the modes of development to craft a song. Our topic is "love" – (groan). I know – it's been done many times. But that is because it is an emotion that is so deeply embedded inside each of us. Let's do a hypothetical brainstorm of that topic using each of the modes of development:

Narration

Let's see. Love of country. Patriotism. The downside of patriotism. PTSD. I will research and find an unusual, untold story of a veteran. My purpose will be to show the affects of war and are forgotten heroes through that story.

Description

How does one describe a feeling? Description usually works best when combined with another mode. I will write a song about how it feels to be in love in Autumn, using the comparison technique of metaphor. Love is the fiery red of autumn (sight), it is the wisps of oak from the woodstove (smell), I brush against it in the plaid flannel of your shirt (touch), it is spice and maple on your lips (taste), it is the whisper of rustling leaves (sound).

Persuasion

First off, I don't want to write about romantic love here. I think I will write about love of place. There is a danger to a place I love. Oh, yes, the hot springs I used to bathe in as a child. They are going to fill it in to make a super highway. I am going to persuade them not to do that. I will use pathos - how that water soothes and heals; I will use ethos - I experienced it everyday, it shaped me, it was a part of me; I will use logos - destroying this spring will affect the eco-system around it and animals and plants will die. Please don't destroy the place I love.

Exemplification

Illustration

Shakespeare wrote, "How do I love thee, let me count the ways." That's good enough for me. I will write a series of "reasons" I love you, and I will make each as personal as possible. I love that you hate mayonnaise and you wrinkle your noise in such a cute way when accidentally taste it; I love the way you tickle my toes every morning as you leave for work; I love that you brush off the car seat before I get in - just a simple list, but a very personal one. My purpose is to show how our love is as individual as we are.

Cause and Effect

Hmm. You know what I'm thinking? We love our comforts in this world. But what price do we pay for them? I think I will write an environmental song. Gee I love to fly, but airplanes emit a lot of carbon into the atmosphere. How much? Gee I love my swimming pool, but what if the entire world had a swimming pool? Would there be enough water to fill them? Gee, I love to drive. But cars are energy hogs and require toxic asphalt roads. Maybe I should drive less. Sure I love my comfort, but at what price?

Division and Classification

Let's see, I already used a little classification in my song saying love is a season. In another song I classified love as love of country. I have written about love of place and love of comfort. However, I want to classify love in its own right. The Greeks had around 30 words to define love. I will focus on the seven kinds of love: Agape (love of humanity), Storge (Family love) Pragma (love which endures) Philautia (self-respect), Philia (shared experience), Ludus (flirting, playful love), and Eros (sexual love). Let's see how many I can get in. My purpose is to make people understand the complexity of this simple word and the importance in our lives.

Process

We human beings are stubborn creatures. It is as if we are determined not to love some things and have to pulled kicking and screaming towards them. It is funny that when we finally experience something, we learn to love it. This usually happens in stages and often surprises us. Recently I learned to love Taylor Swift. First I mocked her for her pretty little teenage girl thing, but then I was drawn to her catchy songs, one step at a time began to admire her music savvy, her persistence, and ability to fend off her attackers and despite all the time in the limelight still is the girl next next door. Ya know, I've taken many steps towards loving Taylor Swift.

Comparison

"Love is like a red, red rose that newly sprung in June" said Scottish poet Robert Burns famously. "Shall I compare thee to a summer's day," questioned Shakespeare. When faced with the song prompt "popcorn" I decided to compare it to love:

> Popcorn's good for you. That's what they want us to think
> it is full of vitamins, anti-oxidants and zinc.
> It gives us energy, is low in calories and fat.
> It's got a bunch of roughage. You know we all need that.
> Love is just like popcorn. It needs a little heat
> but too much heat will burn it
> make impossible to eat.
> Just don't cover it with salt, Or slather it with fat.
> eat it plain and simple. But hey who wants that?
> I like mine at the movies, 1,000 calories
> so absorbed in the flick don't care what's happening to me.
> Love is just like popcorn. It needs a lot of salt.
> If we get addicted we say it's not our fault.
> I read somewhere that popcorn is a better snack than fruit.
> But I know that's a lie, it is no substitute.
> We hear that dear old popcorn is quite misunderstood.
> It's the same with a bad love, we just pretend it's good.
> Love is just like popcorn the right kind is so fine.
> Stay away from the bad stuff,
> make sure you draw the line.
> Love is just like popcorn. It needs a little heat
> But too much heat will burn it-
> make impossible to eat.

Hopefully the comparative techniques are consistent enough to make the point that love is best when we don't get obsessed with it.

Definition

Define love? Well I can't do much better than Corinthians 13:4 –13 (Love is patient, love is kind . . .) so I won't try the general approach. In *Fiddler on the Roof,* Golda sings, "For twenty-five years I've lived with him, fought with him, starved with him. Twenty-five years my bed is his. If that's not love, what is?" Ah, the practicalities of love. In the same vein, I earlier used examples to "illustrate" the things I liked about love. I think I will define love by what it isn't, but I want to be tangible and avoid general words like love isn't selfish or love isn't jealous. Maybe I will go anti-symbol. Love's not a tattoo, a red rose, a blanket, or a "heart-shape" in your text message. It's not something you have carved into your arm in a moment of drunken stupor and spend the rest of your life trying to remove: it's not brief blaze of color doomed to whither and fade, it's not a blanket because blankets yield a temporary warmth and eventually tear and get thin, and must be thrown away; love is not making a little carrot and a number three in your iPhone. Hmm. Ok, that's a good start. Maybe the hook can be, I may not know what love is, but I know what it's not.

And so, now we have taken one word and looked at it from many angles. Using the modes of development reminds us that a topic is not a thesis, a goal, or a purpose. A topic can come from impetus, observation, feeling, or inspiration. There are many ways one can go about shaping your topic. If one way doesn't work for you, try another.

Even if you "feel" your songs and your main objective is to perform them so well that your feelings touch the audience, it doesn't hurt to "think" them too.

Your inspiration is wide and expansive and creative expression needs a big toolbox.

ADDITIONAL EXERCISES

I. USING A NEWSPAPER ARTICLE:

1) Find an article about a topic that is important to you.
2) Write a song using each of the modes of development:
   a) *Narration*: Write a story using personae that is not you. You will need to extract the necessary information and figure out the necessary chronology.
   b) *Description:* Write song in which you use every single one of the senses, being aware of separating your adjectives. You will need to focus on one idea, and the sensory details you choose should support that idea.
   c) Or, combine the two above modes.
   d) *Define:* Choose a term that relates to your topic and that might confuse people, and use aspects from the story to define that term.
   e) *Divide and classify* your topic and write a song on that one narrow point.
   f) *Process Analysis:* Think about a process that will help the audience understand your topic. Chronology is important, as well as an understanding of the steps which created the issue.
   g) *Illustration:* Use a series of examples to get your point across. This might require additional research.
   h) *Comparison/Contrast:* Choose two items that are important to your topic such as two brothers, two lakes, two ideas etc. and using similar language draw a comparison that illustrates your point.
   g) *Argument:* Use an enthymeme to persuade your audience to accept your point. Craft a premise and conclusion based on a second premise you think they will agree with. Decide on a strategy for using pathos/and or ethos.

Yes, that is a lot of writing on one topic, but you will certainly know the best approach by the time you are done!

II. Find an Impetus

A. Consider writing from a song prompt. Timmy Riordan in Boston, MA, runs a Facebook site called, "The Fearless Songwriter", which hosts intermittent songwriting weeks. For seven days, writers write and upload songs based on a daily prompt. Many don't submit complete songs, nor do all participants finish all seven songs. But events like this help give us that little push we need to get going with our songwriting. Practice using the modes of development to find a focus for each daily topic.
B. If you would like a bigger challenge that allows you to pick the topic but requires that you write 14 songs in a month, consider joining the FAWM community. (February Album Writing Month) In the same way as "Fearless Songwriting Week", FAWM gives impetus as well as peer feedback. You can use different modes throughout the month, mixing and matching as the need requires.
C. Look for a songwriting contest that requires that you write for a theme, such as the Pennsylvania Heritage Songwriting competition:

    http://smokedcountryjam.com/?page_id=184%2F

    or the Will McLean New Florida Competition:

    http://www.willmclean.com/index.php?option=com_content&view=article&id=104&Itemid=678

    Contests can be a great deal of fun even if you aren't a finalist and you just might get a great song out of it.

III. REWORK AN OLD SONG

Take a topic that you are familiar with, and perhaps have even written a song about, and think about reworking it from a different angle. If it attempted hard persuasion, think about trying a softer approach; if you used an extended example, try to define a process; if story songs are not your normal route, give one a try. Remember, a topic is not a thesis.

IV. BE AWARE

Start listening for the rhetorical and for the modes of development in other people's songs. You will begin to become aware of how these forms are part of the natural creative process.

PART XV: REFERENCES

NOTES:

[1] Scholes, Robert. *Writing Arguments,*1992.
[2] My research has yet to find an original source for extending the triangle into a rhombus, but it is a form that is included in most composition texts.
[3] Porter, Cole (1893-1964), U.S. composer, lyricist. press interview (Feb. 8, 1955). (Johnson-Sheehan & Paine, 17).
[4] Lesley Gordon, Joanne. *Art Isn't Easy: The Achievement of Stephen Sondheim*, Southern Illinois University Press, Carbondale, IL, 1990, p. 13.
[5] Samuel Clemons to David Watt Bowser, 20 March 1880. http://www.marktwainproject.org/xtf/view?docId=letters/UCCL01772.xml;style=letter;brand=mtp
[6] Proust, Marcel. 1871-1922, *Membrance of Things Past.*
[7] McIntosh, Peggy. *"White Privilege: Unpacking the Invisible Knapsack"* first appeared in *Peace and Freedom Magazine*, July/August, 1989, pp. 10-12, a publication of the Women's International League for Peace and Freedom, Philadelphia, PA.
[8] Lazurus, Emma (1849 - 1887) https://www.poetryfoundation.org/poems-and-poets/poets/detail/emma- lazarus.
[9] Sutherland, Cara A. (2003). *The Statue of Liberty.* New York City: Barnes & Noble Books. ISBN 978-0-7607-3890-0
[10] Robert Connors in his "*The Rise and Fall of the Modes of Discourse*".
[11] D'Angelo, Frank. *A Conceptual Theory of Rhetoric.*

SELECTED BIBLIOGRAPHY

Aristotle. *The Art of Rhetoric.* New York, NY. Penguin Classics. 1992.Print.

Arrien, Angeles. *The Nine Muses: A Mythological Path to Creativity.* New York, NY. Jeremy Tarcher/Putnam, 2000. Print

Batteux, Charles, (1746). Tr. James O. Young. *The Fine Arts Reduced to a Single Principle.* Oxford, England. Oxford University Press. 2015, Print.

D'Angelo, Frank. *A Conceptual Theory of Rhetoric.* Little Brown. 1975. Print May, Rollo. *The Courage to Create.* New York/London. W.W. Norton Press. 1975. Print.

Nadell, Judith and Langan, John. *The Longman Writer.* Rhetoric, Reader, and Research Guide. Brief Edition. New Jersey. Pearson Education, Inc. 2006.

"Statue of Liberty". U.S. National Park Service. www.nps.gov. Web. 20 Oct. 2016.

QUOTES:

We are drawn to quotations for a reason. Some intelligent person has come up with a perfect way to express an idea. The very perfection means that these quotes are often carried from one person to another until the original attribution is sometimes impossible to find.

The quotations used throughout this book were gathered from a variety of sources including print and web, and cross-referenced for verification of attribution as much as possible.

ADDITIONAL READING

Want more about lyrics?

The Craft of Lyric Writing, Sheila Davis, © 1985, Writer's Digest Books, ISBN 0_89879-149-9

Writing Better Lyrics, Pat Pattison, © 2009, Writer's Digest Books, ISBN 978-1-58297-577

Want more about melody?

Melody in Songwriting, Jack Perricone, © 2000, Berklee Press, ISBN: 0-634-00638-X

Music Composition for Dummies, Scott Jarrett and Holly Day, © 2009, Wiley Publishing, ISBN: 978-0-470-22421-2

Creating Melodies, Dick Weissman © Writer's Digest Books, July 1994.ISBN-10: 0898796024,ISBN-13: 978-0898796025

Want to Write a Hit Song?

Six Steps to Songwriting Success, Jason Blume, Billboard Books, ©2008, ISBN-10: 0823084779 ISBN-13: 978-0823084777

Study the Hits: Learn the Secrets of Today's Chart-Topping Hits, Robin Frederick, © Sound Experience, 2014. ASIN: B00O2U9AFA

Writing Music for Hit Songs, Jai Josefs © Schirmer Trade Books, 2000. ISBN-10: 0825672457, ISBN-13: 978-0825672453

Want to know more about the music business?

The Business of Songwriting, Jason Blume, ©2013, Jason Blume. ASIN: B00GA2UDBI

All you Need to Know about the Music Business, Ninth Edition
Donald Passman, © Simon and Shuster, 2015,
ASIN: B00UDCI3RC

The Craft and Business of Songwriting, John Braheny.
© Writer's Digest Books, 3rd Ed. © 2007.
ISBN-10: 1582974667
ISBN-13: 978-1582974668

The Musicians Handbook, Bobby Borg, © 2008, Billboard Books.
ISBN-10: 0823099709
ISBN-13: 978-0823099702

Want the personal approach to everything?

Tunesmith, Jimmy Webb, © 1999, Hyperian,
ASIN: B00HTJMXLO

Songwriters on Songwriting, Paul Zollo, © DaCapo Press, 2003.
ISBN-10: 9780306812651
ISBN-13: 978-0306812651

Want a discussion of the craft, art, and business?

Songwriters' Coloring Book: The Essential Guide to Effective and Successful Songwriting, Bill Pere, © Creative Songwriting Academy Press, 2011. ASIN: B005F50CIK

Want a professional song critique?

Jason Blume: www.jasonblume.com/song-critiques.html
Song Town: www.songtown.com
Taxi: www.taxi.com

. . . and many more! You can find all of the above on that mega-site Amazon.com, (note the ASIN numbers which are Amazon proprietary) but also try libraries, bookstores, and the author's own website for publisher information. As I said in the beginning, there are a lot of books about songwriting. Narrow down the specific issues you would like to find information on, read the reviews, and go to trusted sources and organizations to find the book you are looking for.

ABOUT THE AUTHOR/SONGWRITER

Jane Fallon holds degrees in English Literature and Composition, and Music Theory and Performance from Eastern Oregon University and a Master's in English Composition and Literature from Arizona State University. She has taught English Composition, Business Writing, and Public Speaking at several New England Colleges and Universities for 25 years. In addition, she is an award winning songwriter with 5 studio albums, two live CD's and two books to her credit. She has won the following awards for her songwriting and performance:

Grand Prize Winner, CT Songwriter's Environmental Songwriting Competition
First Place Woody Guthrie Songwriting Competition
First Place, Will McLean Festival Songwriting Competition
2nd Place Great River Folk Festival Performing Songwriter Competition
2nd Place, Ozarks Folk Festival Songwriting Competition
2nd place, Pennsylvania Heritage Songwriting Competition
2nd place, Family Folk Chorale Songwriting Competition
2nd place, Neuse River Music Fest Songwriting Competition
New Jersey Folk Festival Songwriting Competition Winner
3rd Place, Our Santa Fe River Songwriting Competition
Finalist, Southern Florida Singer/Songwriter Competition
Finalist, *Tangled In a Tree,* for Limelight Magazine's Album of the year
Finalist, Rhode Island Songwriters Assn. Competition
Finalist, Mid-Atlantic Songwriting Competition
Finalist, Susanne Millsaps Performing Songwriter Competition
Finalist, Rose Garden Performing Songwriter Competition

Finalist, Solar Fest Performing Songwriter Competition 2011, 2012, 2014
Finalist, Music2Life Songwriting Competition
Honorable Mention: New England Songwriter Competition, Ossipee Valley Music Festival
Honorable Mention: West Coast Songwriter Competition

Jane has performed at venues throughout the country and been selected to perform at The San Francisco Folk Festival, New England Regional Folk Association, Boston Area Coffeehouse Association, The Boston Folk Festival, The Tumbleweed Folk Festival, and the Smoky Mountain Songwriters Festival.

For more information go to: http://www.janefallon.com

More Information About This Project

A companion CD of the music included in *Beyond Reason: Songwriting On Purpose* is available .

The CD includes all of Jane Fallon's original songs that were discussed as examples except for "The Boy He Used To Be", which is on her "Gemini Rising In a Patchwork Sky" album.

Jane Fallon: Vocals
Paul Beck: Guitar, Bass
Jackie Damsky: Violin
All songs written by Jane Fallon
Produced, Recorded, Engineered, and Mastered by Paul Beck of *Lady of Carlisle Recordings*

For ordering information go to www.janefallon.com

"

The aim of art is to represent not
the outward appearance of things,
but their inward significance.
~ Aristotle

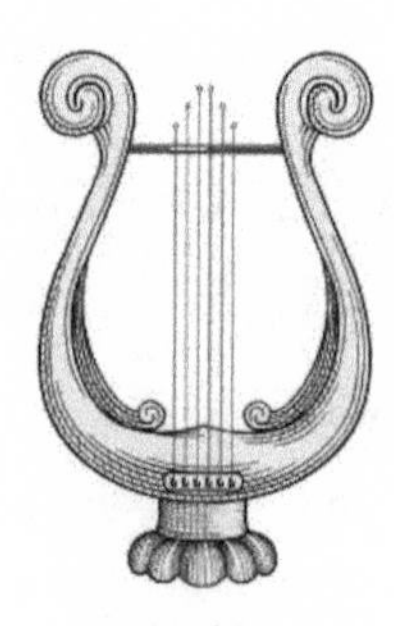

Special thanks to the CT Songwriter's Association (www.ctsongs.com) for awarding the Grand Prize in their Environmental Songwriting Competition to my song, "Northern White." The prize money helped considerably in funding this project.

Thanks to People's Music Network for supporting my first workshop, as I explored how best to present this material to other songwriters.

Also by Jane Ross Fallon:

Seven Songs In Seven Days, a book with music:

"Seven Songs in Seven Days" offers not just good storytelling, but also a few peeks into the creative process of songwriting. By writing and thinking about our parents' pasts, we can better understand the paths we choose for ourselves. This book and CD package should be of interest to those intrigued by personal memoirs, by the father-daughter relationship, by the mystique of the Arkansas migrants of the Great Depression, and by the gumption it takes to craft a melody with lyrics out of thin air." ~ Corrine Smith, Independent Review

Musical CD's:

Faces (1999)
City Girl (2006)
jane plain (2011)
Gemini Rising in a Patchwork Sky (2012)
Tangled in a Tree (2015)

"Jane Fallon is one of the good artists in a world full of soulless clutter." Cyrus Rhodes, Indie Music Magazine

For ordering information go to www.janefallon.com

CPSIA information can be obtained
at www.ICGtesting.com
Printed in the USA
BVHW071920270219
541337BV00001B/80/P

9 780692 796924